Mendel and Morris

Fred Sokol

Copyright © 2011 Fred Sokol

All rights reserved.

ISBN-10: 0615536638
ISBN-13: 978-0615536637

Mendel and Morris began its life as a short story written in 1980.

The novel is published in memory of Sol and Mazie Sokol.

CHAPTER 1

Mendel shook his stick at Morris and warned, "I'll get you next time, you cheat!" Morris doubled over in laughter, his glorious belly heaving as his shoulders rode up and down with each howl. "You may laugh, but to me you are nothing but a cowboy. So, Roy Rogers, go get a horse! And besides, where is Cleveland? Don't answer. You know nothing," shouted Mendel. He knew how to make his best friend Morris laugh and he could not resist. Anyway, what was left for the two of them? More time on the shuffleboard court? Why not enter the next world with a grin? It might please, in his opinion, a Jewish-friendly God. Given all that was going on, it wouldn't hurt to get on his good side.

Morris, meanwhile, a long-suffering asthmatic, reddened, choked, and lost his equilibrium. Fully losing his breath and fast growing crimson around the eyes, he had to be helped to a nearby seat. Mendel returned the corroded cues to the shed, and the weary men sat side by side on the old stone bench. Each looked not merely winded but also bewildered from the long series of matches they'd had that morning.

"Mo, so how long do you think we'll last?"

"Why must you address me in that manner? I am called Morris, like goyisha Horace, but only the rhyme. Mendel, Mendel, you ask me this foolish question at least once a day," Morris replied, his voice not merely stronger but newly resonant.

"Well, what should I talk about – the weather? John Quill, you know, the dean of Springfield forecasters, died a while ago. You want to talk about the King of Siam? He never existed. God willing, sunshine will keep us warm through October. Global healing, I think it's called. Something like that."

"My poor Mendel, this is global heating and it will end the world. Of course, we will never live to see that day. But you, you lead a rough life, what with your sister on the phone with you every day and she looks like George Washington. Your only son and his family visit every so often. Your money pours in from that carpet business of yours. Poor Mendel, I feel so sorry for you." He draped his hand across his friend's shoulder, brushed off a few pieces of lint from Mendel's ragged sleeve.

Mendel sneered and shook free from Morris's grasp. Mendel claimed to be uncomfortable with physical contact, but would selectively allow a hug from a woman he trusted. He welcomed air kisses from old ladies, all the while praying mightily not to have lip connection. "What do you want? You want them to call us, what do they say now, gay?" he snapped. "I wish gay meant what it used to – light and merry….Anyway, for your good health, I would trade that good-for-nothing company and my son and his family. Well, maybe not my granddaughter. You don't deserve her. What good is someone if you never see her -- and money if you won't live to use it?"

"Enough of this talk, you and that Brooklyn accent which hits my head like a falling meteor. Remember that I am just a country Jew, with attitude-light. Yours I wouldn't write home about," said Morris. With contrived deliberation, he lifted his body, by increments, shaking loose the kinks from his massive, sagging flesh and bones, once flexible and resilient in its youth. Morris lifted the shorter, lighter man from his seat, and, with one swooping paw, balanced Mendel before him. "Let's walk, Mendel. This is too good a day to waste with constant complaining. Kvetch to yourself!"

Morris moved forward with a ponderous yet purposeful stride. The frail, slight, Mendel limped noticeably but managed to keep pace with his comrade. "Damn arthritic hip. And it's not even mine. They put in the new one, piece of plastic designed to last five years, and it gives me no relief. Should I live ten years, even fifteen, what then?" Morris silenced him with a tightly clenched fist and threatening look.

Forest Park glistened in the morning sunshine. The old beloved showpiece of the twenties had been spruced up lately, and it made Morris, at least, feel the blessings of youth were not eternally forgotten. He picked up a large branch and mimed, with definition, a quick walk-route, gesturing in the air. Mendel looked perplexed. "Fooled you once again. That's the way the Babe called his shot against the Cubs seventy years ago," said Morris. For the first time that morning, Mendel gave notice of a slight grin. He wasn't beyond a good joke but Mendel, ever tight-lipped, was careful not to often let on.

The two men picked their way through the pine scented woods, descended a hill, turned left along a narrow stream until they reached an out-of-the-way duck pond. The main lake had now become a tourist Mecca, one that Morris avoided. Mendel leaned on a makeshift walking stick, then waved it at the ducks, pronouncing, "Nobody here to bother them except for ancient has-beens like us."

"My crab, you are a friend, my friend, do not besmirch such a glorious day as this with your run-on complaints," Morris declared, gazing skyward in the manner of his onetime favorite actor, Zero Mostel.

"You make a fine and fitting replacement for Hester," said Mendel which caused Morris to roar at the mention of his friend's late wife. Morris never passed on a good line, appropriately used or not. Morris, salivating and coughing at once, again found himself short of breath. This was a treasured moment to be valued and, despite what he imagined was a touch of pneumonia, Morris laughed loudly. He muttered to himself, "I am a victim of my own sense of humor." Morris and Mendel sat.

Morris stood, and raised the reluctant Mendel from his seat. They steadied one another, poised to saunter forward. Two teen-aged girls, midriffs bared to reveal belly-button rings, rode by on bicycles. Morris' eyeballs jumped. "Hello!" he boomed, announcing his presence. The shapely riders waved without looking, then accelerated.

"You think if we cut through the woods we could maybe intercept them later?" deadpanned Mendel, setting off the larger man once again. Mendel bent low and with a few, jagged, exaggerated, elongated strides, made like Groucho Marx – in mock chase after the girls. Soon enough, however, he had to clutch at his ribcage, while rubbing and moaning, "Oy, my aching hip. Why don't they just put me in the electric chair and end it all?"

"Why not? I will tell you. You would complain about the accommodations. That's why not," said Morris, pulling the slighter man along. The two old cronies cackled as they maneuvered. Walking across the lawn-bowling green, the men stood eyeball to eyeball with a stately, unswerving llama. The animal looked out at them from the zoo.

"Some puss you got there, Gertrude," said Mendel. "Who did the surgery? Nip and tuck?" The llama grunted heavily, foamed slightly at the mouth and turned away from Mendel. "Yes, I sympathize," he said. "Next time, use the local guy. You're much better off." He reached up, extended his bony wrist through the rusted chicken wire of the cage, and tweaked the creature just above its malleable mouth.

Marching onward, Mendel and Morris encountered a dozen deer, all roaming freely inside the fence, a dilapidated burro, a hairy water buffalo, and two goats. All were nearly on the sidewalk. Each left in disappointment as the men hadn't the foresight to bring crackers or bread crumbs. "I feel awful, Mendel. How could we forget about bringing moldy pizza crusts? We should be ashamed," said Morris.

"I, myself, can barely walk and, even when I do, my feet kill. You don't sympathize none with me even though you suffer the same way," replied Mendel.

"Let's play one more game. Those clouds, the big ones with ugly black spots, will be here in no time," said Morris, rolling his eyes skyward. He had kept temperature graphs on the weather for a good six decades, claiming always that newspaper charts could not be trusted. Now, he dabbled with websites on the computer but felt secure only with his own data.

"If I can use a second poker as a cane, then I will play with you. Even two games."

"Mendel, you're ahead in the season series. You don't need any cane."

"When my good hip, even, is in its socket. And not, mind you, after I have been for a walk in the jungle here. The nurses tell me I'm bionic and I think they're talking about a plant."

The shuffleboard courts, too, had seen better days, during those times when tournaments were frequent. Now, the concrete around the rectangles was crumbling and the playing surfaces were bumpy. Mendel and Morris, however, approached lovingly, realizing that this was their very own intimate arena. Besides, they had met here several years earlier. Morris moved quickly to the shed, selected a decent cue, still shiny, and handed Mendel a short, pitted one.

Despite his girth, Morris, until the age of sixty, had been an athlete. He played tournament tennis. Catlike in his movements, he exasperated opponents with cuts and slices. He became known for his celebratory, "Game, set, match!" which further antagonized opponents.

Still, he dreamt that he would return, in another life, as a basketball star.

Mendel, on the other hand, played pitch-and-putt golf. Too flimsy in physique to drive a ball more than one hundred fifty yards, he polished a short golf game. He was meant to live on a green. Forever feigning ill health, he would cajole and coax a friend to play with him, then pocket a twenty dollar bill – agreed upon as a wager.

"Bad side and all, I play shuffleboard with you, and this is what I get: a cue that looks like someone stuck it under a flat tire, like a jack." Mendel didn't stop there. "I should know better than to play with anything other than my own model." He had owned a set of cues purchased at a fancy sporting goods store in Manhattan. But, Mendel couldn't remember where the equipment was. Maybe at his son's house in the suburbs.

"Just choose your color, shoot, and zip your lips," commanded Morris.

Mendel gently pushed one black disk toward the ten slot at the top of the inverted triangle facing the players. Morris watched his friend closely, having long been convinced that Mendel actually spoke to disks. The shot swerved at the last moment, skidding to a halt as it touched one of the faded green lines. "Second rate city and this is just one example," fumed Morris. "They can't keep even four decrepit shuffleboard courts free and clear of stones, glass, and whatnot. Young hoodlums bring their dogs here to do business."

Morris stepped up and took a deep breath, as if he were about to shoot a free throw to win or lose a championship basketball game. Then with a looping backswing and blacksmith's strength, he launched the red disk into the air. It lurched and flew, finally tumbling on its side and landed in a far off patch of weeds, well beyond not merely the ten off triangle but the court itself. Morris rumbled, barked, smacked himself once in the chest.

"You're lucky, you Midwestern giant. You caught a break. Otherwise, you'd be in the kitchen! With those muscles, you'll yet hurt someone and you'll lose more than just ten points, but your shirt when they sue you. What do you think this is, the Olympics? Someone gets nailed by one of your shots, but a victim like me gets blamed," lamented Mendel. "I know they'll pin it all on me. It's always been that way."

"Shush, you shyster, always finding an edge to make me lose my concentration," said Morris. But, he began to laugh and winked slyly downward at his best friend in the world.

Opposite styles notwithstanding, the two men were evenly matched players. Each could outclass any of the competition in the park, and secretly, each admired the other's skill. This very day they matched one another stroke for stroke. Neither man came close to approaching the game- winning total of seventy-five points in the early going. After more than a good half-hour of play, Morris began to find the mark, and his score ran into the fifties. Just then, Mendel slipped in a remarkable shot, knocking two of Morris's disks (each ensconced within the eight slot), replacing them with his own black disks. Next round, Mendel picked up ten more points, drawing even with Morris at fifty-six.

"What d'ya say we call it, Mendel? I'm pooped," said Morris.

"This is just like you. No ties in my record book. I am very sorry but, if you quit, you suffer the loss, Mo."

"My friend, I am simply too exhausted to play any longer," emphasized Morris, shaking Mendel's liver-spotted arm.

"I now have one tie in my record book," said Mendel, gazing beyond Morris's shoulder.

Morris, easily holding the cues in one hand, walked to the storage shed while Mendel withdrew from a red, rectangular, soft case two Dr. Peppers, which always followed their matches. Mendel's hands were in the cooler when he heard Morris shouting.

"Mendel! Get over here quickly. Forget the sodas!"

But Mendel had never been one to rush. As a younger man, he dawdled and was always late for appointments. Now, he limped tediously, arriving minutes later. He found his friend on all fours, scribbling frantically on an old, yellowed ripped sheet of spiral notebook paper.

"What is this – a cartoon? Get up off the ground, you overstuffed bear, and show me what you're doing, for God's sakes." Morris, breathing heavily, held the paper up for Mendel to see. Mendel could not make out the letters. He squinted, held his forefinger and thumb together, made a small circle to simulate a lens. Finally, succumbing, he took out his reading glasses, deliberately adjusted them upon the bridge of his once Roman nose, and read:

DOUBLES PARTNERS

SENIOR SHUFFLEBOARD TOURNEY

June 28 – 30

Lauderdale By The Sea

OPEN TO MEN AND WOMEN OVER 65

Write: Mr. Wm. (Bill) Tishman

P.O. Box 71

Fort Lauderdale, Florida

Other: e- mail: ShuffTish@aol.com

"So? It's interesting, aside from that dot com garbage which I do not understand nor will I ever. Now, Morris, what are you doing on your hands and knees?"

"What does it look like? Entering us in the tournament."

"Over my dead body. Play by yourself, play with yourself for all I care."

"And why is that, Mendel?"

"Because I was planning on being dead before this happens. That's why."

Morris grabbed his friend's ankle and Mendel tumbled forward. Morris snatched the smaller man to him and they tangled together upon the asphalt. Morris, simultaneously gagging and laughing, sat Mendel in his vast lap. Mendel struggled to no avail, and finally came to rest. "The only way I can compete with you is to shove you around," said Morris, jabbing his scrawny friend's ribs until even the dour Mendel began to giggle. "Now, are we partners?"

"Partners, shmartners. Copasetic with me but I'm telling you we might as well bring along some pallbearers, too, just in case."

Morris rose, simultaneously elevating Mendel while prodding to shake hands. Mendel did not budge. "My word has been good since the early days in Williamsburg. Besides, you'd probably ruin those few fingers of mine without arthritis – those I use as shooters."

Soon thereafter, they parted, each man retreating to separate living quarters on either side of the park. If not for Morris, Mendel would stay home, content to isolate himself. Above his hallway mirror, he had scrawled, on a piece of lined yellowed paper, "Hermit Crab." A trip to the Jewish deli was an ordeal, a major excursion for him.

On good sunny days, they might meet, just after nine, at the coffee stand. Mendel, delighted to be there, never once let on. Shuffleboard brought each man to life. Otherwise, each realized the feared tunnel, complete with blazing, bright light, might beckon all too soon. Morris had gone to the local library in search of a group he thought was called

"Hemlock Society." When he could no longer shlep his big body easily from place to place, he wanted to be able to take control of his last day on the planet. Morris had committed to memory the proper mixture of gin and barbiturates necessary to take his life pronto, no muss, no fuss. Not only that, he had, years ago, threatened George Goldstein, a crook of a doctor if ever he had seen one, into writing prescriptions for the necessary drugs. Morris, a packrat, kept the papers, which were undated, but signed.

Mendel, on the other hand, had discreetly begun to read books about Eastern philosophy and religion. Contrary to his cantankerous self, Mendel hoped to slip and slide across rather than up or down into the next realm when the time came. He had finally learned that this issue was not to be thought of as a problem to be solved. Previously, Mendel imagined a crossword puzzle grid. If only, he could learn to meditate…..After all, hadn't he been davening long enough?

Back, however, to life, to shuffleboard, the here and now. The following morning, Morris found himself grounded by a torrential spring downpour. "Good for the plants, at least," he thought. "My beloved window box cherry tomatoes may yet yield something edible. On the other hand, that lone red pepper is kaput, soaking or no."

Distressed by the soggy conditions, Morris lumbered about the apartment, flipping through the morning paper to the weather page, which he loudly cursed. "Damn weatherman. There's no risk involved. You predict sun and it rains. So you claim a front, nu, came through. If it doesn't rain, you're a genius. This is a job for which people get paid? I should be so lucky." The phone rang at nine-thirty. Morris kept a full rotary dial telephone in his house; he was old and trusted what was old. Delighted to have a caller, Morris danced a bit as he picked it up.

"So, what are you doing in bed, Gene Autry?" It was Mendel.

"Mendel, hello. You're calling me? Something is wrong?" Morris paused. "No, we just cannot play today."

"Strategy, my good for nothing, is what we need. You think we can't talk up something on a day like this? We need to be prepared. How do we get to Florida and where do we stay? You have, already, these answers?"

"Well, no," said Morris. "We have time to plan, don't we?"

Mendel replied, "I am at the coffee shop and I bought you one of those goyisher raspberry danishes you like so much it must remind you of some girl."

"Give me 10 minutes to dress and get there. And be quiet!" Morris yelled.

"With my hip, I'm not going anywhere. Don't worry, I'm sitting here reading the Daily News."

"Stop complaining, just for once," commanded Morris. "At least, wait until I am able to k-nock you one."

"Good-bye."

Obsessive in their quest to be tournament competitive, Mendel and Morris played shuffleboard each day for the next month, spending up to four hours a shift at the courts. Most of the time, the pair concealed their intent through individual challenges against one another. Mendel filled a tattered record book, noting individual, season, and career match results. Every so often, they'd find a twosome to play. The truth was that Mendel and Morris couldn't find much competition in the park. And, in their age group – over seventy or even over sixty? Forget it.

But, they needed practice. Theory was fine and they'd actually researched the sport. But, Morris boomed, "Practice, practice, practice....tradition, tradition." That's what they needed. Playing as a duo, against opponents who didn't know the first thing about stopping or blocking a disk, was a bore. Their own individual combat sessions proved more productive even if steely silence inevitably permeated the concluding moment of each encounter.

So it was that one June morning after the heroic twosome had easily played through a few matches with casual friends, Mendel chose to speak his mind. "Morris," he said, "we have to get out of here. Let's move. We can play that tournament in Florida and many more. Why not settle there? Here, I'm not having much fun anymore and neither are you. We don't even fight right at this point. If I can't get a doozy of an argument out of you, what good is our friendship? And those other so-called players? We are without anyone who can knock us on our ass."

"And what exactly do you mean by any of that?" asked Morris. "We have train reservations, on Amtrak no less, for three weeks from now. What now, you want me to sell the tickets?"

"And you are a cockeyed oaf? Always, you want something new. You are sick of this life and I am the one content to die. So, this is just something we need to set a fire under each of our seats. Go no, let's switch positions." Mendel tapped the ground with his cue, rhythmically driving home his points.

"Such an orator you've become, Mendel, a regular wheel. Soon, you'll clobber me one, over my poor head, with that stick," said Morris, his eyes beginning to roll and twinkle at once. "All right, then. I'll take care of the car rental for tomorrow morning. Or, is that pushing?" he asked, swatting his friend across the back, sending him sprawling.

"But, what about AAA, which neither of us has? AARP will do no good at this point. Besides, I drive maybe once a week, not more than ten miles in the past month. I need practice," said Mendel.

"Just in case, bring at least three sets of glasses. You never know when a cheap magnifier might help out, even when you're driving. Those are for reading."

"Morris, for your information, it is not too late for me to back out. You are one enormous horse, but do not trample on me," Mendel warned. As they left the park, though, Mendel stooped no longer. Instead, he strode forward without the slightest trace of that limp, upon which he so often blamed any misfortune.

For the next several hours, the men separated. Each was busy with last minute details, compounded by lack of travel experience during recent years: packing, cleaning, phone calls here and there. Not only that, there was email to check and, possibly answer. Neither man could understand more than two computer related commands or functions. But, they wanted to keep up and secretly each wished for greater literacy than the other. Time passed as each man twisted and turned his way through the night.

Morris arrived at his friend's home before dawn the next morning only to find Mendel, stuffed suitcases lined up on the front steps, practicing his stroke with a broom and saucer on the porch. Morris lowered his car window and shouted out, "Out now, you whatdyacallit, Brooklyn Dodger, you! We're on our way!"

"An Oldsmobile, no less. Didn't you read where they went out of business and about time, if you ask me. I had two, one the old sedan with the jug taillights, the other a Cutlass, no less. Each a lemon. You might as well have bought a hearse for what we'll pay in rental for this gas guzzler."

In no time, nonetheless, Mendel had locked up the house and tossed his bags (grips he called them) into the back seat. Morris gunned the motor and sped away from the old neighborhood without taking even a moment to glance back.

Morris, insatiable in his many appetites, was certain that he could drive forever without taking a break. He made quick work of Massachusetts, Connecticut, New Jersey, Delaware, Maryland, and the District of Columbia, stopping only when it was essential. Yet, it was with resignation bordering on remorse that the large man pulled over and suddenly said, "Mendel, I'm not so young no longer. Take the wheel before my eyelids make mincemeat out of my pupils."

"I might have known you would save the South for me. So, if the Klan appears with clubs and knives, you will be snoozing. I suppose you want me to deal with those bigots. Is it that you somehow think I look less Jewish than you? Is that it, Moishkie? What if I just drive over that bridge into Virginia and look for some two-bit motel? I think I'm ready to sleep, too."

But, Mendel was talking to no one. Morris had fallen off immediately and Mendel, more confident when he fooled himself into believing he was alone, drove on for an hour before pulling off at an exit highlighted by a "Holiday Inn – This Way" neon sign. The hotel was nearby and Mendel jerked the car to a halt in the parking lot. As he did so, the snoring giant, who had wedged himself in between the seat and dashboard, awakened with a start.

"Mendel, Mendel, where are we, in the South? Georgia?"

"I'll give you Georgia. Compared to New York, it is. But, no, not really."

New millennium or not, the hotel lobby was early 1950s, featuring shades of yellow and green colored vinyl couches. A smiling youthful receptionist welcomed them with an enticing, "Hi! Mighty glad to have you boys at the Inn!" The buttons of her blouse strained to release her.

"I'll give her an in," muttered Mendel who mumbled something to himself. Morris poked him so hard in the ribs that grimacing Mendel clutched, with both hands, at his side. It seemed he might fall to the floor.

Morris sucked in his ponderous paunch while Mendel quickly pushed the few remaining gray strands of hair he still had on his oblong head from one side to the other, then slicked them down with saliva. He threw back his shoulders with a snap and proclaimed, "And we are mighty glad to be here!"

"We are en route to an athletic contest further south," added Morris. "We need rest and a good workout room in the morning."

"Oh, do you have tickets? Is it a baseball game?" asked the wide-eyed receptionist.

"I will have you know," said Mendel, "that we are competing in a tournament in Florida."

"Why, how nice," she responded, a touch of drawl now apparent in her speech. "A senior event, I'm sure. Well, how can I help you men out?"

"First, we need a double for the night," said Mendel, trying to sound casual.

"Uh, you mean a room with one double bed?" she asked, winking, then wetting her orange lips and subsequently smiling at Morris.

"Well, no, we want two rooms with a double bed in each," he said, flicking his eyebrows with embarrassment.

She thumbed through a bound "Holiday Inn – Stay With Us" notebook. "Yes, we happen to have two perfect rooms for you boys. Only thing is we don't have anything together. One's down the hall, not far from here actually, but the other's on the second floor. What do you say, boys?"

"I got the one just down that way, Miss. With my arthritic hip, which actually doesn't bother me much at all, I'm still better off staying on the safe side," Mendel said.

A visibly perturbed and rattled Morris elbowed Mendel. "Thank you, Miss. We'll take the two rooms and decide in a few minutes who gets what. I happen to favor the lower berth myself. So, if you'll just leave us be," said Morris, reddening again.

"Anything for you, anything you boys say," she replied, handing them forms to fill out and key cards for the rooms. "I'm on till six in the morning if you need anything more. All you need is to pick up the phone if you want me. Me, I'm Breanna. Have a nice night." And she licked those delectable lips once more and turned away.

"The health club, where is it? I will visit first thing in the morning. Got to keep in shape," Morris said.

"You just call and I, personally, will escort one or both of you," said Breanna.

Morris appeared at the desk just before six in the morning, having slept soundly but briefly, his pattern following obsessive driving. He had barely placed his head upon the lumpy pillow when the glaring sun's rays began to stream through the chintzy transparent curtains. Before shaving, Morris thought he might take a turn on an exercise bike. He crept out of the room, tiptoed down the hallway, and made for the front desk.

There, he found Breanna, wearing nothing but what he thought was a bra, even though Morris knew a more appropriate term must exist for the elastic band she had on. No matter. The contraption barely covered her chest and fully exposed her taut midriff, highlighted by a silver stone in her navel. Morris, astounding himself, was aroused.

Breanna leaned forward on the counter, seemingly unaware that another human was within earshot, and read a glossy magazine. She rested a tiny strip of belly upon the desk. Suddenly, she swept back her golden hair with one hand and turned it into a knot at the back of her head.

Ever the gallant, Morris cleared his throat. "Miss, excuse, Miss, but would the gym area be open?"

"Oh, it's you, Mr. Morris. Well, yes, that is, soon. In fact, that's where I head when this extended shift is over, in about three minutes. You're probably wondering about my outfit. I always hit the machines, for some aerobics, before I leave. Then, when I'm home, I sleep better. You should try it. Or yoga, even."

Morris was dazzled. He genuinely wished to make eye contact with this enticing Bree, about whom he dreamt. He could not, however, force his eyes. So, Morris glanced over her shoulder at the wall clock. "When you're ready, lead, and I will follow, just as I used to do many years ago dancing. I was never any good at directing the girl. Forgive me for rambling on."

Breanna, at the top of the hour, came away from her station, and Morris had to steady himself. He didn't really want to look down at her but could not desist. She wore skin-tight shorts. He had no idea what they were called. "Follow," she said, and he, hoping his swoon wasn't obvious, pursued.

Morris tried to keep pace with Breanna's canter as she loped down successive hallways. She stopped at a door marked "Spa" in large black letters which Morris found easy to read. Breanna pressed various buttons before popping open the door.

Morris felt encased in glare. The fluorescent overhead lights instantly bathed the white walled room with simulated sunlight. Morris watched as Breanna quickly snatched a couple of bottled waters from a cooler. Then, she took Morris by the wrist, led him to a machine and asked him to sit down. Morris did as instructed.

Morris thought that she had the wrong name. It didn't fit. Better if it were shortened to Bree, even better change the B to F so you have Free. That's what she was -- Free, like the basketball player he used to watch: World Be Free....

Basketball had been Morris's choice of sport, more than tennis, even. Over six feet tall and always burly, he had been able to play center, even into midlife as he patterned his game after the great George Mikan who perfected sweeping hook shots with either hand. Morris used to stand in front of a mirror, pivoting on one foot and then the other as he mimed release of a basketball toward an imaginary hoop he envisioned upon the ceiling. Morris thought himself a true gym rat, having once befriended a high school custodian who cut him a key in exchange for some phone numbers.

Now, he was inside a health spa which had a sheen like Bree's hair – it was nearly platinum. Again, she circled Morris's wrist with her thumb and third finger and led him to a machine.

"You watch me. This is what you need," she said. Legs slightly splayed, she grabbed for a handle above her, then twisted forward at the waist as Morris felt a mixture of anticipation, embarrassment, and self-loathing. For, he was certain that Breanna, her chest heaving in and out in perfect rhythm, would soon spill out and over her top. Morris could not decide where or how to look.

Exhaling, she remained relatively under control, pointing toward her stomach and then at Morris's midsection. "Now you."

Morris thought of Mendel who could beg off, back out of such a predicament claiming various phantom aches. Morris, still vain and egotistical, would not be denied and so he positioned himself and grabbed above for the bar as Breanna said, "Go for it, but slowly." Morris felt his doughy gut ride forward as it slid over his belt but he managed the stretch without incident.

Straightening up, however, something below his belt harshly tugged on him and Morris knew he was in trouble. Still, he feigned comfort. When Breanna signaled to the next station, Morris was forced to admit, "I think maybe my muscles are a little unaccustomed and tight?" He thought it might be a good time to use Mendel as an excuse. "I think, Miss, maybe I should call my friend Mendel. But, thanks." Breanna remained silent. She was not used to men, of any age or shape, bypassing the opportunity to watch her work out. "I will be back and then you'll see something," said Morris.

"Whatever," said a totally perplexed and puzzled Breanna.

Morris made his way to the elevator, then up a few flights to Mendel's floor. Although in pain, Morris managed to tiptoe along. A light sleeper himself, prone to awaken if someone sneezed hard next door, Morris assumed the same of everyone else. Arriving at Mendel's room, Morris rapped on the door three times. No response. Morris put his mouth to the door and shouted, "Mendel! Up!" And then more softly, "No fooling around. Besides, some Miss America is in the workout room." Still, no noises from within. Morris briefly considered breaking down the door, something he had accomplished at a cheap motel, much to his dismay, years earlier.

Instead, he proceeded to the registration desk and asked to use the house phone. He rang Mendel's room. Five rings and then a message advising that "this guest is not answering." Morris asked the new clerk, a man this time, if he had seen Mendel. Pressed for a description, Morris said, "Small, old Jewish man. He looks like he might have been a tailor, what with his slouch and walk. But, he's wealthier than that. If you knew him, you would be shocked at his success in life." Morris added, "He looks like an ancient crane, you know, a bird, a bird with a cane."

The clerk suddenly perked up. "Yes sir, I've seen your friend. He's right in there, with Lucy. Came wandering out here a while ago. Said he couldn't sleep."

"Lucy?"

"Another one of us, sir. You know – young, pretty, bright pink lipstick, and a blue bow in her hair. Curves." He spread his hands apart, drawing a silhouette in the air, and Morris knew.

"And this lady, what would you say, is she forty or fifty years younger than my friend, maybe more?" But as he said so, Morris thought of Breanna in the spa. "Seven in the morning and he's having breakfast with this Lucy?" With that, Morris turned and rumbled toward the motel restaurant.

Astonished to find a swinging door at what he considered a swanky joint, Morris pushed it open angrily, nearly setting a waitress on her ear, and cleared his throat before speaking. "Mendel, my friend, your hip hurts you so that you are able to entertain this Lucy, who is lovely, at this hour?" Lucy blushed and Mendel, sneaking glances left and right, shushed Morris as best he could. But Morris kept going, "I tried your room as early as six thirty," he lied, "but there was no answer. None. The day man sent me here."

"Morris, my friend, my partner, my confidant," Mendel began, "Lucy and I were talking. God strike me dead if I am fibbing but it was nothing more. I could not sleep, my back hurt so from the mattress. Still, I am in pain," he added, reaching around for his tailbone.

"Never, or may the real, actual God strike me dead, will I believe that story," said Morris, staring at the pretty lady and, occasionally, at Mendel.

Lucy was quick to recover her poise and, dabbing her lips, tried flirting with Morris, whose mind was stuck in the health room. "Why, sit right down. You're an awfully large man. So, rest that weary body right here."

"Yes, Morris, sit. Have a cup of coffee on me." Mendel spoke quickly now. "I went to the front desk to get some Maalox. My stomach, you know. This sweet young lady was kind enough to sit and talk with me. I'm an old man, Morris," he said, wincing.

"That's all, I'm sure," Morris said.

"C'est tout, sugar," said Lucy, flashing Morris a sly, toothy grin.

"Well, if you are that old and decrepit, maybe we should skip this tournament which, may I point out, is our reason for traveling to a faraway land."

"Morris, not here. I mean, I'll be better soon," said Mendel, coughing as he pressed both hands to his sunken chest.

Just then, the room began to sway to the beat of loud, amplified music. Mendel manipulated his bony fingers across his shriveled, pointy ears and shrieked, "If you are up there, what's to become of me? Cannot I die in peace?"

Lucy rose and took a moment to smooth back Mendel's remaining stray, stringy, scattered wisps of hair which he'd carefully raked over from the side of his head. She looked at Morris straight in the eye and said, "'Lectric guitar, honey. Bye for now." Off she wiggled, intent to mingle with the group of flashy, second-rate musicians.

Mendel, sagging, picked at his toast while Morris gulped down two cups of scalding coffee. No liquid was ever hot enough for Morris, who sat down, dwarfing his chair, sighing like a rhinoceros. Mendel opened his mouth to speak but the roar, followed by the howl of laughter emanating from Morris's chair, overwhelmed them. Breakfasters turned as Morris began to shake. His laughter sent his entire frame into spasm. Finally, Morris collapsed in a massive heap.

Mendel's creased face cracked like old pavement. "Just what is so funny?" he asked as a slow, complacent grin spread across his lips.

"It's just that you with your bum hip and that luscious Lucy. She could be, easy, your granddaughter. And, we're going to some sandy beach in Florida, but I ask why? Mendel, Oh Mendela, what will become of us?"

"What will become of me is my business, not yours. And you might as well say oy, not oh, it sounds better – more appropriate, just for your information."

As they left the dining area, Mendel blew a kiss to Lucy, briefly setting off his large friend once again.

"Excuse me, I have some unfinished business," said Morris to Mendel. "You pay the bill so when I come back we can blow this joint." Mendel nodded.

Morris walked directly toward the spa, stopping only when he reached the front door to study advisory diagrams. He forced himself to stare at a certain image. The picture showed a man who looked, to Morris, to be in great shape. Yet, this man, so said the caption, was wondering whether to "rid himself of love handles, trim his gut, firm his abs, increase his pecs." Morris, realizing he needed a glossary to even understand the terminology, entered the room.

Asked if he needed help, he said, "Breanna, please," and was directed toward a whirlpool area set off in a separate suite situated far beyond the weight room. "I will always remember you, thank you," Morris said, his eyes upward, recognizing that Breanna was alone. Morris reddened. He thought she might be naked.

"I am here to say good-bye but to share the hope that I will see you again," he said.

"Mo, it's been my pleasure," chortled Breanna. "Take my card," she said, lifting one out of a waterproof case with plastic ducks inside. The floating tote rested upon the side of the spa.

"If only," Morris began, but he didn't need to complete his thought. Breanna was smiling and waving. Morris understood this to be the finale.

Morris knew why he felt better but in no way would he let on to Mendel. Soon enough the pair rejoined for the long drive. Morris seized the steering wheel and never let go.

Despite their differences, Mendel and Morris shook hands in agreement. The journey, itself, was reward enough. Who cared about results? They did. This particular trip would be deemed a success only if it allowed them to reach their destination – in this case, Fort Lauderdale, and the publicized shuffleboard tournament. Speeding south on the interstate was nothing new to these men. Foliage, landscape, topography was of no regard. The territory was familiar, recognizable.

Only once did they attempt to break tedium by playing a game, the object of which was to spot the oldest car on the road and identify it immediately. Not surprisingly, the contest led to dispute. Mendel persisted in claiming the 1948 Hudson, with the antique plate, was the winner since that model was no longer made. Morris, interpreting the rules according to his own standard, insisted that a 1950-something Chevy he passed put him over the top. In truth, the men did not care for competing against one another. They argued on and off for hours before resolving the situation by declaring a tie.

Every so often, Morris stopped the car as each, protesting any need, made his way to the rest room as quickly as possible. Neither ate even snack food. The sight of pre-cooked hamburgers and semi-stale pizza left them cold. Even Morris, known for typically consuming great quantities of food, his and anyone else's, abstained.

Seventeen hours after leaving the Holiday Inn, the men, weary and famished, reached their destination. Having left the northeast impulsively, Morris had not thought to book accommodations ahead of time. He correctly anticipated that vacancies would abound. Neither Mendel nor Morris anticipated the scene awaiting them once they set foot upon what had come to be known, in Fort Lauderdale, as "the strip."

Lining the sidewalks across the street from the ocean were hotels and motels of all sizes and quality. Mendel motioned to a smaller place with a sign that read:

INDOOR & OUTDOOR HEATED POOLS

SHUFFLEBOARD

COLOR TV

AC

"That's our joint, Morris."

The big man nodded his approval. Registering quickly, the men made their way to their one large room, with two double beds. Moments later, each lay fast asleep.

Time slows its beat in Florida, with acknowledgment to the rhythms of the elderly. The junior-aged and their parents, the super-aged (who now live well past ninety in many cases) with reflexes having grown somewhat less responsive, are most thankful. Hoping to outwit the gods, Mendel and Morris would rise daily, stretch limbs, and, thinking of athletes he idolized, approach the shuffleboard courts. Oblivious to heat and humidity, they would practice and practice.

Mendel complained that he could not endure the length of even one full game, such was the nagging, biting arthritis in his hip. Soon, he insisted that his entire side was impossibly sensitive. Morris, on the other hand, having lost his playful and comic edge, grew suddenly rude and mean. Disrespectful to those blatantly inferior, he was boorish and unpleasant on the court and elsewhere. Morris openly questioned the decision to travel south with Mendel.

The men became immersed in a physical and psychic struggle for survival. Morris and Mendel quarreled with one another about: the weather, the cleaning woman, the paltry hotel breakfasts, the slope, and, relevant to shuffleboard, even the paint job on the courts. As competitors, however, their game reached a pinnacle. Playing doubles, they couldn't be stopped. No one was able to touch them, and few even dared.

The temperature suddenly rose into the upper eighties before lunch and Mendel felt the sun scorch his skin. Morris, ignoring his own human vulnerability, blustered on. He, too, though, lost the bounce in his step.

Baring their backs to the tropical sun for a quick match, then taking a sudden dip in the pool, the men bantered easily with those sitting on lounges. This was their contact with the outside world. Otherwise, they stayed inside, blasting the air-conditioning to the max, speaking to no one. By the time tournament week arrived, the men, wearied and spent, would have been delighted to take a train home. Neither had actually voiced the impulse, fearful of the other's response.

Upon their arrival, Morris had called Bill Tishman, whom they deemed pretentious for having the audacity to leave an email address. Tishman, affable to the point of being cocky, said, as if in a rehearsal hall, "Yes, I'm Tish, 'Southern Regional King' they called me until rheum took over. Now, I only play exhibitions. Yes, more than glad to have a couple of Yankees on hand for the upcoming show. You're the M&M boys as far as I'm concerned. Might as well be Mantle and Maris."

Humbled for once, Morris managed, "Thank you and see you on the big day," before hanging up.

Soon enough, tournament day was upon them and Mendel and Morris slowly made their way toward the site. Mendel limped markedly as if to deliberately exaggerate while Morris dragged his whale-like body along the sidewalk. This route held no mystery to them since they had checked it repeatedly during the previous month.

Bill Tishman sat at a rickety bridge table. Surely, it and he had once been transported from the Northeast. Tish welcomed all players and while he had never met M &M, he was certain of their identities.

"The Bronx Bombers or my mother did not name me William Tell," he said, extending his left hand while remaining seated. Tishman, it appeared, did not recall the previous conversation.

"I'm Morris Kahn, from Cleveland, and this is my partner, Mendel Greenbaum, from Brooklyn."

"But we live in Springfield, Massachusetts as of this moment," added Mendel, shrugging his shoulders as if he could not explain just why.

"I know from your handwritten registration forms," Tishman said, his tone of voice clearly judgmental. "Most people these days email or fax. You boys are obviously not up to date. But, we won't hold that against you," he said, even if it was obvious he had already designated Morris and Mendel losers. "That's my wife Sadie, over there. You boys married?"

"Both widowers," said Mendel.

"Sorry for being insensitive," said Tishman. Morris and Mendel could see that Tishman was a liar.

"It has been too long for each of us," said Morris, closing the topic, at least for the moment. "What do we do now? Are we on soon?"

"I'm pleased to say that you will play shortly. I have you matched against those two women practicing on the third court. Sadie, introduce the M&M Boys – won't you, dear?"

"I'd love to, Tish," she said, shooting him an icy glance that would cause a thief to pause in the act of pilfering. "Follow me, boys." Off she went at a slow but steady jog. Neither Morris nor Mendel could keep up and Sadie slowed as she glanced over her shoulder.

Moments later, she sang, "Girls, your competition is here!" Mendel thought of Gertrude Berg, who happened to be Sadie's role model during the early 1950s. Sadie, gesturing with both arms, drew the opposing teams near. "Gilda and Zena Lewis, I would like you to meet Mendel and Morris or is it Morris and Mendel. Uh, I don't really know their last names. But, Morris is the, ah, big one," she said, reaching up to tap him on the shoulder. Morris didn't mind which prompted Sadie to squeeze harder. The players exchanged greetings and the men were given fifteen minutes to warm up, to get the feel of a new court.

"I'll be back soon with the official for your match," said Sadie, and away she went, her legs churning.

The men had purchased new cues in Miami. Contemporary items, however shiny and spiffy, were not to be fully trusted. Having broken the sticks in well during the past weeks, Mendel and Morris had some confidence in the equipment.

Mendel limbered up cautiously, careful not to strain himself – further. How could he have possibly developed a kink in his right side while sleeping? Morris, on the other hand, was tense. He pawed nervously at his crotch. In between practice shots, he scratched and prodded himself. Morris's strokes were out of control. Moment after moment, he sent disks flying beyond the ten -off rectangle and toward the benches beyond the court. Mendel, meanwhile, could not recall even a measure of coordination. Finally, he took one, last feeble shot, his perception so cloudy, eyeglasses slipping to his chin, that he barely grazed the seemingly elusive disk.

In a flash, Sadie arrived back on the scene with the referee, a wizened man with a scrawny, gray mustache. "This is Murray, what's his name, one of our best." Murray doffed the gold golf cap he was wearing, revealing a badly fitted brown toupee which rested near but not completely upon his skull.

Murray flipped a coin and the women won the toss. Morris sneezed so loudly that it seemed, to Zena, an intentional tactic designed to distract. These were women whose partnership was seasoned. Quite accustomed to tournament play, they shot first. Gilda slid the red disk forward fluently and it inched to the center of the ten-point triangle where it stopped, as if drawn by a magnet.

Mendel tried to straighten himself but instead wobbled awkwardly, lost his balance, and grabbed awkwardly for Zena's arm to prevent an embarrassing fall. Upright again, he cleaned the tip of his new cue, and shot, once again nearly toppling over. The black puck flew directly at Gilda's red one but then, unaccountably, as if caught in a mini-gale, missed its primary target and skidded off the court. Mendel muttered beneath his breath, shrugged his bony shoulders, and sat. Zena rose, positioned herself precisely, with her posterior protruding, and shot. The disk whisked to the left corner of the court, and stopped short.

"Good eight!" shouted Murray, at last finding his voice.

Which unnerved Morris. He took a stiff-legged, wide-spread stance, remembering Joe DiMaggio at the plate, and gave that pill a mighty shove. Whoosh – crash!……against the low wooden frame serving as a border for the court.

Mendel looked scornfully at his partner but allowed a tight-lipped grin to creep from one corner of his creased and lopsided face to the other. "If I had your body, Morris, I would save it. Never, never would I waste my strength with such a shot."

The game was over in less than twenty minutes, the ladies trouncing Mendel and Morris by thirty points. The men rallied to salvage the second of three in overtime, seventy-eight to seventy-six. Zena and Gilda remained cool and nonplussed. The men were stunned.

The final game would determine all and the girls were certain they would triumph.

The tie-breaker proved no contest. Gilda and Zena, urging each other on with hand signals they had not previously utilized, wiped out the Springfield Jews by forty-five points. Mendel couldn't keep out of the "kitchen" – he hit the ten- off box twice in succession, three times in all. Each time he yelped as if speared in the stomach.

At the end, massaging his aching hip, he had to halt play once in order to swallow a pill. Morris shot with explosive force and corresponding lack of accuracy. Within an hour, Murray was lifting the sisters' joined hands in victory.

Attempting to follow protocol, Morris and Mendel, profuse in their compliments, congratulated the ladies. Soon enough, visiting Tishman for the last time, they signed the official Players Book, and walked off – to sulk. With their cues dragging behind them, they trudged on in silence.

A block from the motel Mendel broke the ice. "I am sure we overtrained. We had those broads, I know it in my bones. I don't know what happened. Morris?"

"We lost. They won. They were sharp, we were not. End of story. Kaput."

"My hip, though, it cost us the last match. Maybe I should have seen a doctor. I couldn't shove off right."

"Shove right, shove left, shove in, shove out, you were never any good at this. So, quit your bellyaching."

"The money we spent on this trip, each of us would put it to much better use. What do they say on the television, one and done?"

"Mendel, you spent a lot for this. Me, I didn't have that much to start," said Morris, who looked off as if distracted. Sometimes he talked without paying attention. His wandering left eye, however, indicated lack of interest.

"What, cowboy, are you thinking of?"

"Nothing much, just that those two girls are not the worst looking I've seen. And, no one's been banging down our hotel room doors. You know, the one with the low crouch and the big beam, she's not so bad looking."

"She just happens to have attracted my fancy, too," said Mendel.

"With your hip, it would be a total disaster. I can see it all now," Morris replied, gurgling, laughing, holding both his sides at once.

"You think you're such a big shot, you, with your Midwest accent. Don't think I don't know that you bring it out whenever you need to impress anyone in the room."

Nodding in unison, Mendel and Morris slapped their palms together, a gesture they held as secret as a handshake. Helping one another to the hotel, they quickly showered, changed, and made their way back toward the courts. Mendel dismissed the surprised Tishman with a quick, sure wave. Morris questioned Sadie who politely informed him that the Lewis sisters had a match, thirty minutes later, on court one. The boys slapped hands once again, with Morris giving much more than he got. Mendel grimaced with mock pain but no one paid attention.

The men climbed the three-layer bleacher behind the court. There they sat alert, newly aroused, with their eyes on their former opponents. Morris suddenly elbowed Mendel in the ribs, nearly knocking him over, and said, "Mendel, do you – I mean, suppose they're not Jewish?"

Just then, Gilda and Zena came into clearer view. Mendel, having had cataract surgery and Morris, opting for that newfangled lasik procedure, could each see more clearly than in many years. It was a struggle, however, for either of the revved up seniors to maintain a modicum of poise. Anticipating and fantasizing with the fervor of forgotten adolescence, each man, in his own way, primed himself to the ready. Mendel pulled his red Arnold Palmer golf cap across his matching sunburned skull. Morris sucked in his stomach with one mighty breath.

Silence.

They surged forward in anticipation. Life would now begin.

CHAPTER 2

Gilda and Zena had lived in South Florida for the past fifteen years. They were currently renting a cozy house in Coral Gables. It backed up to a golf course but that was of no interest to these women. They spent much of each year in transit, moving from town to city, traversing the state, signing in at one shuffleboard tournament after another. The itinerary kept them hopping, with little time for idle thought. The two men agreed this was a blessing.

Now, having disposed of the final twosome in doubles, the ladies collected a handsome trophy, another item to carefully store in a cardboard box, and gathered their belongings. With cues, stickum, towels, wristbands, and unused sunhats packed up, they walked swiftly away, just as Morris and Mendel approached.

The boys began to pursue but Mendel slipped while hopping down from the bleachers and turned an ankle. His gaze focused upon the retreating Lewis ladies, he claimed he could no longer walk.

"Nu? I've carried you before, Mendel. My only problem is what will people think down here. Well, if they don't like it, too bad for them.

Drape your arms about me and hold on with your dear life. I didn't work as a lake lifeguard for nothing for five years, maybe more. So help me, I cannot remember."

"These days you don't look so much like the matinee idol guy in that black bathing suit who sat on the lifeguard stand. Second, just give this ankle bone five minutes to heal and maybe then I will be ready. Must you always be in such a rush, where's the fire?" asked Mendel.

"It was my definite impression that you, you and me, that the two of us were hoping for, attempting to make conversation with those women. We agreed to tail those women or am I going deaf?"

Mendel looked directly at his tender foot, shrugged his shoulders, pursed his lips in pain, and then smiled. Everyone watching the match had left the area. Tish and his Lady Sadie ambled off. Only Murray, the introverted official, remained. Murray was quick and physically sure, but he could not bring himself to make a call. Morris wondered what in the world Murray was doing trying to pick up spare change as an old people's shuffleboard ref. It appeared that Murray was cleaning the courts, as well. No one was waiting for Murray, the custodian.

"Hey you, umpire!" Morris shouted at the wiry janitor.

Murray rose from his hands and knees. He had been diligently eradicating a stain created by a Coca Cola spill on a nearby court. "What is it?" he asked, in a refined tone of voice.

Suddenly self-conscious about his own dialect, Morris said, with care, "Why do they stick you with this good-for-nothing job? A man such as you should not be spending his valuable time cleaning up fools' messes."

"It's not so bad and, besides, keeps me busy and my mind occupied. What else could I do?"

"I cannot answer that but you look like a man who should not be asked to wipe up what some slob has spilled on concrete. I don't know what else you could do but listen, come over here, I want to ask you one question."

Murray approached carefully, avoiding contact with any of the painted cement. He treated the courts as if they were shrines, to be forever pampered, and regarded with honor. He took a circular route, affording Morris a moment to quickly whisper into Mendel's ear, "You should know nothing funny is in my mind about this Murray. Just advice I'm offering."

Mendel replied with gusto, "Never do I know what you have up that oversized sleeve of yours. Suddenly, it's my business too?"

"You care about these courts like they were your family," said Morris when Murray arrived.

"I have neither much of a family nor anything else, I suppose," said Murray. "So, yes, these courts they plug a hole for me," he said, and pulled down his fisherman's cap. "You guys must get around, no? How about sharing a secret or two with another geezer?" asked Murray

"Ha!" laughed Mendel. "We must put on some good show. You should see me in the tub, what with my two point landing – such a thud you never heard. This is some lollapalooza of a project. I tell you so, so big." He shook his head in self-mockery.

Morris, who already had Mendel within an arm's length, reached for Murray. The official offered no resistance to the grasping Morris. Morris sat on a bottom bleacher rung, holding two skinny, yielding but otherwise completely dissimilar old Jews on either side of him.

"The fact is this, Murray, that despite what a learned man might call my bravado and despite my friend Mendel's charm, we are surely just as lonely as you are, maybe more. So, you can do us just one favor, a mitzvah. What can you tell us of those adorable Lewis girls?" he said, his eyes rolling backward in his head.

"Oh, oh ho, now I get a clear picture. Gilda, Zena, are you interested in them? Hard sisters to reel in, but worth it, I will tell you. They live together in the same house and it's been that way for the eight years I've been down here. Hey, you guys got your work cut out if you got the hots for the Lewis girls."

"Murray, we got all kinds of people up north," said Morris. "We can fix you up anytime you visit. Just name even your type – fat, not so fat, whatever. Just give us a lead so that our time down here is not a complete and total waste. We need to find them."

"This much I know," answered Murray, 'To thine own self be true,' it's from Shakespeare. Anyway, they stay at The Flamingo which is just off the beach. But, you have to be quick to find them. They can get a move on when they want to. Well, I hope this information is of assistance." He gracefully doffed his cap, bowed deeply and theatrically, showing sparks of animation which Mendel and Morris could not have anticipated. Just as swiftly, Murray, the chameleon, the shifty one, transformed into the beaten-down cleaning man. He turned, and growing perceptibly older, stumbled toward a far court, his gait slow and stiff. "Can't slip death's call," said Murray.

Morris ignored this and said, "A wonderful bow, Murray. I'll do you one too, Murray." Morris leaned over…but had trouble straightening up even three-quarters of the way.

"Now, at last, my green giant of a friend, off to find those alluring ladies," said Mendel, lifting his limbs as if readying for take off. Remarkably enough, each man had rhythm and a hint of bounce to his step.

While Mendel and Morris thought the other more decrepit, neither could dare to imagine life completely devoid of the other. In this regard might they have been newlyweds. The specter of a more isolated existence, for the M& M boys, was frightening. A glance toward lonely, solitary time held no promise. What, after all, of the abyss awaiting them? Day-to-day survival was problematic enough.

Now, though, they perceived a cornucopia, a time blossoming with radiant flowers, delectable fruits and even an occasional drink. If this was short-term, why not enjoy it for its worth? They sashayed up and down the strip examining more modest motels and seedier joints, too, before boasting to each other of their own good fortune. Still, no Flamingo.

Mendel asked the hot dog vendor, who also had soda, ices, and even some prepared sandwiches. "Mister, you know the Flamingo Hotel?"

"I got the finest hot dogs this side of Nathan's. And Nathan's down here is nothing to write home about. The Flamingo, the bird you mean?"

"Nathan's in Brooklyn, you mean?" asked Mendel, more animated now.

"As I said, I don't count the ones down here, on Long Island, in Yonkers, fast food Nathan's in airports. I got the genuine thing. Here, take a bite."

Mendel did just that, then bought a couple of franks for Morris and himself. "You got something here but you're nothing but a boychik. How come you know so much about Nathan's?"

"My father ran the original, managed it, so help me, for fifty years till he died. That was his life. He could smell a non-Kosher hot dog two blocks away. So, I have a small place down here…and this cart. It's not a lot, but respect I do feel."

"I need to see you get a storefront." Mendel pointed both thumbs downward. "This cart is nothing. A kid could sell these. Come on, you can do better." Mendel realized that he sounded like the hot dog peddler's father even if he and the seller were close enough in age.

"Mendel!" roared Morris. "If he doesn't know The Flamingo, let's not, shall we say, tarry. We are wasting precious moments and they have, no doubt, moved on."

"Don't mind my friend," explained Mendel to the frank dealer, "Morris, he's practically goyim. From Ohio, no less."

The vendor, this new friend who had slicked back his thick gray hair Elvis-style, with the duck ass convergence in the back, wanted to talk. He poured Coke into cups for Mendel and Morris in an effort to detain the twosome. Thankful but eager to get on their way, the men drank quickly and left.

"We are just a bit in a rush. You don't know what this might mean if we find the girls?"

"Don't I?" said Mendel. "Do you think it was some twin of mine that, not to be cute here, turned a trick with that little Lucy?"

"You should be ashamed."

"My advice to you, at the time, would have been to stay in the health club with whoever it was, Miranda or something. But you didn't ask me, so you lost out."

Morris, without responding, prodded his friend forward. They walked all the way down to the swings and basketball hoops but still no Flamingo. Mendel was dragging his leg by now but Morris was certain his friend's pain was in his mind rather than the body.

"Listen Mendel, let's go get a phone book. That way we'll know for sure whether this Flamingo actually exists."

"You go in that place over there," said Mendel, pointing to SURF AND SEA, ETC. "I'll just sit across the street under the palm trees. Come and get me."

Morris returned a good while later with both a telephone directory and several sheets of paper. He skipped around cars at the heavily trafficked intersection. "Mendel, I found no Flamingo. They were good enough, though, to work some computer magic. You won't believe this but I did turn up one Mildred Flamingo, Coves Rd., Ft. Lauderdale. Don't ask me how they got this out of the computer, but here it is. Maybe she's the one."

"Can't be the one. Murray told us they lived down by the water."

"You trust a guy like Murray, over the hill, someone who no longer looks forward, a man stuck in his scrapbooks? He probably knows little or less and besides, for all we know, she lives around here. Look at all those streets, it would take us a day to cover them on foot."

"Hand me the book, you lug," said Mendel. "I know how to sweet talk a woman – women of all ages. Get me on the phone with her and off I will go. You wait."

"Not on your life. After I left you the last time with some dame, look what happened. I have no trust in you. You and me, the two of us will call."

"Fair enough," Mendel answered and they walked back into the restaurant, keeping distance from one another.

A whiff of 1950s décor at SURF AND SEA was more than enough for Morris. The place was plastered with wallpaper featuring brightly colored dinghies, buoys, and ropes, scenes too good to be true for mid-twentieth century America. He had to admit, though, that the place did smell like the sea – salty and stale. Morris, ignoring a small voice in his head urging him not to remember, found himself immediately transported to another time and place – his many years as a fatigued, distressed, robotic encyclopedia salesman. Walking door to door, he never believed the spiel he had memorized. Always, if only he could maneuver his way inside to sit down, he could sell those World Books. Otherwise, holding fast to a suburban storm door, he didn't have a chance. No matter what, he could not come up with enough dough to support the family, at least in the style he hoped. They didn't complain but whatever it was inside of him, did they call that alter ego, wouldn't shut up. Never did he feel adequate. But, that was another time. He wished he could channel amnesia. He also wished he had never, ever sold door-to-door.

Mendel snatched the phone quickly out of Morris's hand. "Hello!" yelled Mendel, too loudly into the phone after someone answered. "Hello!" He turned to Morris. "Someone said something but I do not know what. Now, I am waiting and nothing." Just then, he heard a distinct voice. "Yes, someone's here. It's Mendel Greenbaum."

"Never heard of you," was the answer, the exasperated response. "What do you want with me and don't say you have a small island available for $1,000 cash. First I don't have it and secondly I want to strangle you if you are one of those talk-quick-think-of-everyone-as-dumb telemarketers. Am I clear?"

An irritated Mendel composed himself instantly. "Is this the Flamingo Hotel? By chance, are you the owner?" he asked.

"This happens to be my home and I am currently installing a system which will effectively screen out junk callers. You have reached Mildred Flamingo and I have been here since my Herb passed on. Sometimes my daughter Anna stays here, that is when she's not managing one place or another. And lately, my younger sisters. Before I cut you off, what business is it of yours?"

Morris had to wedge in a word. "We were wondering only since friends of ours are staying at The Flamingo but we couldn't find the joint."

"I don't doubt it since I am the only Flamingo here, as far as I know."

"Morris, it's them. They were here," said Mendel.

"Now, is that all you want before I hang up on you?" asked Mildred Flamingo.

Mendel jiggled the phone. "If it's not too much trouble, we would like a number for your sisters. They beat us in a shuffleboard match and we were hoping to congratulate them. So, Mildred, can you help us?"

"Who are you and why are you calling me by first name? I don't like that or you to start with," she screamed.

Morris interceded, "We were actually just hoping to find their next tournament date. They are enjoyable, given their significant expertise, to watch. Do you know when they play again?"

"No, I don't, and I won't help," she said, slamming down the phone. Morris shrugged, Mendel stomped his good foot, and everyone else observed.

"Mendel, we'd better go off somewhere to eat. This heat and that conversation don't agree with me so good."

"What time is it? I can't see the hands at all but maybe this is six o'clock. Correct. We have not eaten one bite in hours. But, we need a strategy to intercept those girls."

"Who are you, suddenly, James Bond? I don't know how I ever got hooked up to such a Casanova?" Morris asked no one in particular. "All right. I'm ready for anything, even something which makes my stomach turn. I suppose at our age, why not?"

This time, it was Mendel grabbing and pulling Morris along. "For once, close your mouth and follow me. We're off."

Too soon, they were doused by an unexpected downpour, sheets of rain drenching the pair. Soaked to skin and bone, Mendel and Morris, a road show team, began to laugh. It was a dissonant enough duet: Morris coughed and bellowed deeply while Mendel cackled in the falsetto he never would acknowledge.

"Turn your back in Florida, it's raining," spat Mendel. "Spin around or, in my case, wobble, the sun's out again and blistering the stretched skin, no less."

Morris, an expression of certainty spreading across his face, looked down upon his partner. "Another windmill, my friend?" he asked and, without further hesitation, they were off in pursuit of Mildred Flamingo and, more optimistically, her two recent house guests.

Wringing wet, characters out of a comic strip, they began to jog, to limp down the avenue. In-line skaters, bicycle riders, frustrated Lexus and BMW drivers, fast-walkers, serious runners, and young parents with children in tow, all splashed their way somewhat aimlessly but nevertheless joyfully. Morris and Mendel, odd complements to it all, smiled again and again and once again.

Just then one particular cloud opened up and burst upon the heroic pair. Momentarily children, they welcomed the onslaught as if this might be the worst natural disaster they would ever face. Of course, it might very well be the last. Bedraggled yet undaunted, they moved along the sidewalk, then took a bolder approach to walk at the edge of the beach.

The waves nearly lapping at his feet, Mendel remembered fondly the drive to Coney Island, Rockaway, even Jones Beach. The years in Brooklyn, after all, provided what the world now referred to as perks. A man who feigned ignorance of the late twentieth century not to mention the twenty-first, Mendel was a closet futurist. He had investigated cryonics, thinking that just maybe he would like to reappear someday when medical science caught up to his dreams.

Now it was more than sufficient, as he gazed into the turquoise ocean water, to recall the Cyclone, a ride which neither thrilled nor frightened him. Or, the long tunnel which led from parking lot number four at Jones to the salt water pools and the burning platinum sands. To Mendel, the ocean, which he imagined stretched forever, was rejuvenating, a possessor of infinite possibility. He felt he might just jump a wave. Such a move would leave Morris dumbfounded. Mendel was certain that Morris believed he, Mendel, was an incurable pessimist who lived in constant dread of his mortality. In reality, Morris thought Mendel was physically falling apart. Morris blamed Mendel's hypochondria for his sorry state of mind.

Mendel swiveled, took a sudden right angle, strode purposefully onto the surface and belly-whopped into the Atlantic. Morris, incredulous, could do nothing more than shout after him. "You'll drown, you weasel. You can't swim, you can't do even doggy paddle. You're meshugge, crazy like a loon. I don't know you. Come back here before I have to save you."

Mendel began to undress. He was down to his white boxer shorts as he paddled out to sea. Then, on his back, he waved to Morris and a growing contingent of onlookers. "This is life!" he yelped. "Now look who's on the downward slope, you slug, you."

Morris paused to collect himself, reluctantly admitted that it was Mendel who had stepped out, leaving Morris damp in the sand. He realized that Mendel was speaking the truth although that comment about the downward slope, lacking in innocence, felt mean and cavalier.

It was, however, true. The topic of choice, for Morris, was the ledge. How to bring it up? From this spot, he would fall, tumble, or even leap at any moment. Could he trust his friend enough to confide in him? After all this time, he could not figure Mendel – how to reach him. Should he extend to Mendel – or not?

Instead of ruminating further, Morris, as he hacked furiously through a couple of lackluster waves, went in after Mendel. When he reached the back-floater, Morris, spitting salt water said, "This will be the end of you. You'll catch pneumonia. And look over there," he instructed, as a bolt of lightning shot across the sky, darting at the whitecaps.

"Morris, you sound like me, with your complaints. You say I got problems? A little water never hurt even a single soul. Besides, when those ladies hear stories of what we went through to find them....of vicious ear-splitting thunder and menacing flashes of lightning, if that doesn't impress them, what will?"

For Morris's benefit, Mendel began to stroke backward, toward land. As if he had been composing the line for hours, he turned toward Morris and said, "You speak of souls. I will my soul, may it live unto all eternity, to this ocean."

Caught off-guard, Morris, walking through thick waves to keep up, could not reply. Instead, he shook his head slowly but deeply, as if to signal agreement.

Mendel continued, "You, me, our friends still with us, we want always to solve the problem or find the answer. It's never when we die, but if. And if, where do we go? Assuming it is possible to devise a plan which promises a better go of it next time through. Instead, we should float along. Look at me now – do I look troubled?"

"For a wet fish, although shriveled, you don't look so bad. It's what you're saying that is so crazy. You got a bad faucet, you fix it. You want to talk afterlife, don't spin in circles. Make sense," finished Morris, pleased with himself.

"And you, for a walrus you'll pass," said Mendel. "Look out!" he yelled and Morris attempted to dive, headfirst, beneath a wave. Not more than fifty yards away, a shard of lightning split a beach umbrella, snapping it in half. Morris struggled to regain his footing.

"Mendel, this might be the end of me. Before I go, I want to find those women. When they discover what we've gone through, they won't be able to resist us." And with that, Morris pulled off his shirt and tied it around his waist.

"Look at him roll!" shouted Mendel, to no one in particular.

"This device will help me stay above the waves," explained Morris.

Gradually, the two men made their way to the shore. As soon as Mendel's feet touched the ground, he began to limp. Morris, on the other hand, gained momentum as he marched along. "Morris, let's stop at that Howard Johnson's, which must be the last remaining one of its kind."

"After you made fools of us both at the Holiday Inn, I'm supposed to blindly walk right into another embarrassing fiasco? No, we are going forward, now that we're back on track. Don't you realize that if those girls were headed anywhere, this storm has, without a doubt, stopped them. We must reach The Flamingo before they leave."

"Provided they'll even see us, okay," said Mendel, the skeptic.

"Just for five minutes, out there in the sea, you were something of a sleek fish, a trout, a baby seal....whatever lives in that chartreuse water. Now Mendel, I see you for the crab you've always been."

Mendel suddenly lost his footing but then, as if walking a balance beam, recovered and regained his balance. Windmilling his arms, he hailed the only cab in sight.

"Now what?" asked Morris.

"I'm getting dry and then for me it's off to Cove Road and Mildred Flamingo. If you care to, join in the fun. If not, may you drown in peace."

The cab pulled up, Mendel fell in and Morris followed. "After you," said Morris.

"Pull your shirt on, big man," said the driver. "Company regs, you know."

"I'm wringing wet," said Morris. "It won't fit."

"Not my problem. I'm nearly off duty. Seats stay dry, you gotta cover yourself. Okay?"

It took Mendel's assistance to pinch and prod Morris's flesh into the Arnold Palmer golf shirt, by now a few sizes too small.

"Quit grabbing my skin," scolded Morris.

"I am grabbing your fat," said Mendel. "You look like a wet, stuffed animal, Morris," said Mendel. Each man grinned and Morris covered his mouth.

"Be quiet, shush. You're disturbing a driver at work," said Morris.

The cabbie meandered through the empty streets, jerking the car around corners, swinging blind turns out of memory. The M&M boys tried not to notice the shabby state of houses as the drive continued. At last, they pulled up to a white stucco house badly in need of a paint job. The exterior plaster appeared to be cracking further by the moment. An iron stake lay on the front lawn. Resting upon it was a fake pink flamingo -- elegantly perched, but uprooted.

Mendel dropped a ten dollar bill in the cab driver's lap and the men, stiff and sore, emerged from the vehicle. Mendel could not fully straighten his upper body. He felt permanently stooped. Morris, the complement, fell forward before recovering his balance.

"Mendel, we should have gone back to change. Look at us, like some drenched animals caught in the storm before entering an ark." Morris furiously twisted the bottom of his shirt.

"For a giant, you got a small brain. I will, though, remember this about an ark and someday get back to it," said Mendel. "You know the real enemy – time. Always we get older. We cannot go backward, especially for the sake of fashion. And look at that sky. This is Florida, not the North. A few minutes and she'll dry us good, like some oven or even an electric clothes dryer on heavy no less. I'll bet you. We stay wet and I buy hot dogs for twenty days in a row. If I win, though, you got to lose twenty pounds by next month. Plus this: whoever loses can no longer kvetch quite so much. What say?" asked Mendel, elbowing the larger man in the midsection.

"I say you're right about time. We'll be dead and gone in how long and then no one will care about any of this. If not, you keep me going. Now, let's make the acquaintance of Miss Mildred Flamingo." And up the front porch they sauntered.

Mendel rang the bell as each man took a step backward. Before they could shy away, however, a tall woman whose straight, yellow hair hung down past her shoulders came to the door. She wore a tight fitting knit dress which accentuated her shapely chest and narrow waist. Mendel and Morris, equally flabbergasted, stood and gaped.

"Pardon me," said Mendel. "We're looking for someone older, Mildred Flamingo. We must have the wrong house."

"I'm Millie," the woman said, pushing her rose-colored sunglasses to the end of her nose.

"But, you might as well be Marilyn Monroe for all I know. A movie star or some singer, somebody we saw on TV," said Morris.

"You don't sound like the Flamingo I talked to an hour or two ago," said Mendel. "And you certainly don't look like her."

"Mendel, act your age. Be polite before the lady," said Morris, turning to Mildred. "He is so lonely he sometimes speaks before thinking. Age."

"Maybe you spoke with my mother. She's Mildred, too. One of us is always around, you know, for business," said Mildred Flamingo.

"So, you two are businesswomen?" asked Mendel. "What do you sell?" He eyed Morris.

"I hope you can forgive my friend who looks like he's falling apart. He still has a mouth and a nose both too big for their own good."

Mildred Flamingo seemed receptive to Mendel's query. "Come right in and I'll show you around. You boys looking for a room for the night? The week?"

Morris replied, "There is no doubt that we could use better accommodations."

"We rent out rooms. Look around for yourselves." As they entered, she looked them up and down, making them nervous as she scrutinized. "On second thought, come around to the back patio. You look drenched and that little squall could not have done that to you. I'll get you something. Ice coffee or tea? Hot coffee? You look frozen, maybe you boys need a shower?"

"Well, even if it's ninety degrees outside, I'm cold," said Morris. "Come, Mendel," instructed Morris, once again acting as if he were tending a little brother. They followed Mildred Flamingo around back where several citrus trees, clustered together, seemed to welcome the old men. Branches opened wide. Hanging oranges and grapefruits brought a smile to Mendel's face. But, the small fenced-in yard was, more appropriately, a children's plastic playground. Mildred had a tiny swing set, wading pool, and rectangular sandbox, bounded with rubber borders on all sides.

Whenever he was perplexed, Morris raised his left eyebrow, stopped, and considered. Mildred observed this, then anticipated: "They're for my grandchildren – my daughter's two little ones," she said.

"But, you're not old enough," said Mendel, not finishing his thought or sentence.

"Nearly fifty is plenty old. I've been nipped, tucked, embellished, and augmented. You name it," said Mildred Flamingo. "Only my surgeons know for sure," she smiled.

Mildred placed two steaming cups of coffee on the glass table. "Yes, we do run a boarding house here. And, under typical circumstances, I would tell you we're booked. For big boys like you, though, I would rent out one of my own bedrooms in the main, the proper part of the house. You interested?"

"I say we didn't see any sign out front," said Mendel.

"Well, truth is we only rent to people we know," said Mildred. "I imagine that sounds crazy but that's the way my mother did it. Now that might be backwards business sense, I mean in terms of profit, but that's it -- we just hold that line. So, we're either booked up or we lie to people since Mama doesn't want just anyone in here."

"You have clientele now?" asked Morris.

"Two women?" continued Mendel. "One who is thin or trim, the other endowed, maybe zaftig, if I may, you know, a well-rounded person?" he asked and blushed fully.

"As a matter of fact, yeah. You know Gilda and Zena?"

"They plastered us all over the shuffleboard court. The semi-finals. Nice women, though, aren't they?" questioned Morris, innocently.

"They're my aunts, my mother's sisters," said Mildred.

"Well, to come to the point, we would like to wait here for them, wherever they are," said Mendel. Morris, looking skyward, could not believe what he heard.

"I don't see why not," said Mildred, pleasantly. But, they're out for dinner – down on the strip, if you want to know – Sam's."

"You're sweet," said Mendel, drawing her to him with that same irresistible look which helped him to score on the road trip to Florida. He kissed Mildred on the cheek, doffed his floppy cap, and added, "That's what we needed to find out. Now, we run," he said, as Morris mouthed words but said nothing.

"You're welcome to stay for a while with me. I'm not doing anything much," said Mildred.

"Don't extend invitations with him around," cautioned Morris. "With ladies, he's faster than he looks. If he were a woman, you would call him a fox, if you know what I mean. Especially for his age. Don't let his looks trick you."

"Well, anytime," said Mildred, "but preferably not when my mother's around." She whistled the letter s. Mildred sashayed away from the men, went back through the house, hips swiveling smoothly as she waved to them over her shoulder.

As soon as they were out of view, Mendel jumped into the road to flag down a cab. The mission was now clear: get back to the motel, change into something more presentable and flattering, then search the strip for the Lewis girls. Could they possibly accomplish all of this within an hour or so?

They rode back swiftly, found some snazzy outfits and dressed clumsily but quickly. M&M then walked to Boulevard Diner, a likely spot. No luck there. Despondent, they thought of giving up and actually began to make their way back home. Mendel suddenly stumbled on a patch of broken sidewalk. Morris hoisted his tumbling friend to his feet just as Mendel, head tilted, noticed a familiarly triangular building just a block or so away. Once a House of Pancakes, it had become SAM'S KITCHEN. Mendel and Morris were frequent customers.

Sam Goff, in and then out of retirement, purchased the old place three years earlier. He renamed it, in his own honor, immediately. Having previously managed first one, then a chain of IHOPS in northern New Jersey, he was at ease. Besides, at seventy-seven, he wanted more money, not a poolside chair at a generic condo development. Although the sign attached to the entryway had changed, Sam kept the basics of the old menu. No logo, same pancakes and six containers of syrup. He also added: lox, bagels, corned beef, pastrami, and even gefilte fish. He presented soft diet foods for those coping with dental duress. Sam's became a hot spot, even a haven for old folks who had settled in south Florida. A good deli helped Florida seem just like home.

Sam, himself, always drew a crowd. Long ago, he had been a featured actor on commercials during television's early days. Kids called him Mr. Brylcream. Sam was versatile, able to create minor magic by snatching quarters out of kids' ears. Spend time with Sam, you were sure to return, regardless of the food he served.

Mendel and Morris, certain that Sam's was the place for them, were pleased they had changed into spiffy, color-coordinated shirts and trousers. As they stepped into the restaurant they immediately spotted Gilda and Zena Lewis in a corner booth. They were irritated that Sam Goff was entertaining the ladies, probably, Morris imagined, with kids games, no less.

"Two Jews, two boy Jews, boy, not goy Jews, as Sam I am," cackled Sam, his gravel-like voice cutting through the crowd. "From the land of Ted Geisel and Green Eggs and Ham, no less, are these, my kinsman." He glanced from Zena to Gilda. "These young fellas come in each morning but never, until this very moment, have I seen them past noon." He turned to Mendel and Morris. "Be my guests. And meet the Lewis girls who, most often, settle in this very booth, opposite me, for Early Bird each afternoon."

"So, this is where they get their strength," muttered Morris, to himself. "Pleased to make acquaintance, again," he said, addressing Zena, his woman of choice.

"Yes, for nutrition, not certain about seeing you again," said Zena, who, nonetheless smiled broadly, revealing a gap between her two front teeth. Morris thought about his onetime best friend, Ernest Sternberg, who could have caught a fly between his two prominent choppers.

Sam interjected, "I wouldn't trust a man like Mo on such a flimsy chair. Might break, he could sue me, although you wouldn't try that, would you? And I don't want a cracked piece of furniture neither. Pull up that other chair, the one with the big arms, will you? Now, don't tell me you seniors know each other?" asked Sam, feigning innocence.

"Sam, mind yourself. These gentlemen are excellent shuffleboard players," said Gilda. "I am delighted to see you boys once again. But, why are you here?" she asked.

"Well, I mean our motel is nearby. We've been in for breakfast and thought we might take a chance on dinner. Unless he changes cooks, these guys serve up a mean pancake, twenty-four hours if I have it right. Morning, noon, and night. Reminds me of the all- night joint we used to go to after bowling, in Cleveland, years ago."

"The big one's no fool," said Sam. "My chef don't really wake up till afternoon so by now, he's flipping those griddle cakes with his wrist." Sam demonstrated by turning his own, hairy forearm upside down.

"Not to change back, but you people have played shuffleboard together?"

"Actually, just hours earlier today," said Zena. "Call us friendly opponents."

Mendel broke his silence, "Listen, that's easy enough for you to say. Those girls are out of our class, Sam," he said.

"That much I knew without even a mention of shuffleboard," said Sam, laughing at his own attempt at a joke while everyone else simply sat still. "I mean, I ask you?" But the line fell as flat as one of the pancakes.

"You boys are from Springfield, Massachusetts, a city never reborn, is that right?" asked Gilda.

"How did you know? And, why do you have information on Springfield?" asked Morris, leaning across the table, which began to tilt as he applied pressure.

"Tish told us that you were very good, and that you came from an old New England mill town," said Zena.

"Part of that is true. We are currently Springfield residents. The rest I don't know, judging from recent events. You two wiped us up on the court, that much cannot be disputed. No match for you two. Otherwise, we've been alright," said Mendel.

Zena plucked a stenographer's spiral notebook from her handbag and began to sketch. Mendel peered over his eyeglasses to see what she drew. Within a rectangular framework, she created what seemed to be a long road, until Mendel realized it was actually a river. Zena created hills on one side and old Victorian house frames on the other. She added cumulus clouds. Finally, she took pains, erasing as she worked, to represent a long, tapering church spire.

"Okay, I give up," said Mendel.

"We used to drive to Vermont once every summer when I was growing up. My father was one of the lucky ones to have a car even if it didn't go much more than forty miles an hour. It seemed speedy at the time. Before that god-awful interstate highway was ever created, everyone took back roads up from Connecticut. This is what I remember of Springfield. For me, the river always stood out. It was bounded by hills, homes, and fluffy clouds, at least in July. I have a painting, saved from those years, and currently hanging up at home."

"You're an artist?" asked Morris.

"First realistic, now more abstract," she answered. "An artist from Brooklyn, no less."

Morris said, "My friend, without the manners, he's from Brooklyn, too. Why you have poise and he has none, that's what I am wondering."

Gilda said, "We lived there until maybe 1965. Those were times when we weren't moving around so much."

"Mildred, your niece, supplied us with days you travel. We thought we might not even catch you," said Mendel.

Gilda seemed irritated. "And why were you speaking with Millie?" she asked.

"If you must know, Morris and I wanted to find you two. She provided answers," said Mendel.

"Some sister she turns out to be," muttered Zena.

"No, we mean the younger, you know, curvier Mildred," said Morris. "With what do you want to call it, the nice build or am I offending? Not that the older one isn't. Well, we haven't yet met your sister."

"You've probably said enough, Mr.?" Asked Zena.

"Kahn with a K. Morris Kahn and he's Mendel Greenbaum."

"Do us a big favor and leave us alone. We catch a bus in a half hour," said Gilda.

"I know my cue and I am out of here," said Sam. "As an old summer stock actor, which I was for too long a time, I can sense a moment. You four fight it out. I'll be in the back. Whatever you want, hotcakes, lox, call me. On the house." And with that, he turned on his heels and made a beeline for the kitchen.

Morris was in need of rescue but by the time he turned toward Mendel, the smaller man was uncoiling himself like a repressed serpent. "Two old men need company. Do you ladies think about the next world? I do, as does this whale of a friend I have next to me. That is all. We don't know anybody down here and the two of us, after fifteen minutes, go after each other's throats. I mean, spending every moment with him, I need a break. And he probably feels the same way.

Don't be mad. We're aggravating yes, but not that bad. So, let's have coffee?"

Gilda looked skeptical. "We got not much more time here. I understand, Mendel, what you are saying, though. Zena?" asked Gilda.

"I am always the one to get on someone's nerves so, with that, I apologize," said Morris. "No, not to you Mendel. You lovely ladies cannot find time to share a meal with a couple of old goats like us?"

Zena cleared her throat and rose, as if delivering a formal speech. "All right, but order quick," she snapped, like a drill sergeant. "Digestion might be limited but that cannot be helped."

"I have no system, anyway, if you know what I mean," bellowed Morris.

"If you paid some attention, maybe you wouldn't carry so much weight," admonished Zena. With that advice in hand, Morris ordered four pancakes with maple syrup. "A Danish and coffee, make that black and scalding, please. This is good," added Morris.

"Look, I realize that you two are Queens of the Court, but you know everything about diet, too? As for you (he gestured toward Zena), you eat like a bird. No wonder you're too thin. I can see your ribs."

The four of them sat silently, eyeing one another, taking stock of prospects. Zena knew that Morris, given a bit of attention, a measure of affection, might be some catch. Sure, he was a good fifteen, twenty, maybe more than that, pounds and a couple of belly rolls too much to handle, but she could take care of that. She'd had the practice. And Mendel, thought Gilda, was a charmer. Hume Cronin-like, he sat back before speaking instead of taking center stage before he was welcome. His crooked smile, she thought, matched her own. Strange to like someone because of the bite of his teeth.

Morris, whose long marriage had been less than ideal, was more forgiving of women than was Mendel, for whom no one would measure up to Sadie. Morris ignored Zena's twitch, her tendency to interrupt, and her proclivity for pointing an index finger when she spoke as if, eventually, she would pounce and puncture someone's side if she kept at it. Mendel thought Gilda pleasant and articulate. She was more reserved and non-obtrusive. He imagined sailing away with her, even if he had never been aboard anything but a sunfish, and then only for the ride. Still, he envisioned guiding the boat while she admired his dexterity.

Morris, visibly nervous and unable to sit still, yelled at Mendel, called him "a stubborn little nothing." Morris did not want to make the trip back north since he had no desire whatsoever to go home. Mendel responded with a declaration that he was staying put. He mumbled something about splitting up. This made no sense since the men were in accord. Still, Mendel continued: "I am staying put in Fort Lauderdale."

Finally, Zena said, "Enough of the loneliness in your lives. You got each other, that's something. When you're through with self-pity, we'll talk with you. You both would feel much better if you weren't so sorry for yourself."

"You're the one to talk," said Gilda. "She's the one who was never satisfied with a man and she's the one who complained about our mother. That's not to mention her daily aches and pains."

"Stop that!" snapped Zena, growing beet red. Morris, admiring her glow, allowed his imagination free rein.

Gilda turned to her sister. "Would it be such a crime if these guys came with us to Miami, maybe as cheerleaders?" She then faced the men. "We play in a tournament at some swanky hotel, The Royal Palm I think it is."

"Are you crazy? We don't want them since all they would do is distract – us and everyone else," said Zena. "I'm sorry, boys, but this is our tournament and we registered way ahead of time."

"And what would be so terrible if we entered mixed doubles?" asked Gilda.

With that, Zena lifted herself up, straightened her shoulders and back, inhaled, and took her sister by the arm. "We have to use the pink room," she explained. Mendel sat stiffly, picking at a stray cuticle while Morris gobbled up a second portion of food. Sam soon came by to check on the entourage and Morris shoved him toward the Ladies Room.

Mendel and Morris simply sat and gazed beyond one another's shoulders. The men realized they couldn't challenge fate. Not when they were quite so mentally or physically exhausted. Mendel was certain it had all been pre-determined anyway, so why huff and puff. Sadie and he should have lasted a lifetime. She was taken away early for some good reason, he didn't know what. Why push for a replacement when he would rather live with memories of his sweetheart?

Morris, on the other hand, knew only that he had to win over a woman. Always, he saw himself as the controller, the boss. That many relationships during his long life had been temporal and failure was clearly not his fault. Of this, he was convinced. It was always someone else's problem and, assuredly, her fault. Now, he had dual purposes: snag a good woman for the rest of his days; and, when he left this planet for the next, reserve prime turf for the subsequent run.

Mendel and Morris had each fallen asleep. They were jarred awake as the girls returned. Zena spoke first, "Come to Miami with us, play doubles with us, but you (she touched Morris's stomach), do not follow me twenty-four hours, is that clear?"

The men, still groggy, were delighted. "All right, boys," said Zena. "Get yourselves and your grips here within an hour. We'll take a late seven-thirty bus to Miami. Be here or be square!" she commanded.

"This one is for me," muttered Morris, mostly to himself.

Mendel said, "Too good to be true. Perhaps someone up there actually looks after us?" He glanced at the ceiling, hoping no one would notice his gesture. Mendel had long ago severed his association and belief in a higher deity. His father had been Orthodox and, having spent much of his youth in shul, he rebelled forever more. Mendel boasted that he was not really Jewish and he certainly did not observe. When an outsider took potshots at Jews, though, watch out! Now he seized the opportunity to impress and blurted out, "Maybe there really is a God!"

Morris was equally astonished. Down on his luck and remarkably indecisive for a man of such bearing, he said, "Why? Why are you asking us?" before Mendel could continue with his thought.

"Maybe my older sister got dibs on common sense or she just always had brains," said Zena. "Let's get moving. Practice rounds begin tomorrow. We're staying with friends and I'm sure they'll put you up or find another house. After that, who knows?"

"Sam, bill us," commanded Gilda.

"Whatever the girls say," said Sam, pleased with himself for having arranged what appeared to be a double match. "When to next expect you ladies?"

"A month or less -- not long," said Gilda. "You're a regular mensh, you," she added, tweaking the restaurateur's cheek.

"One of you, just one, if I would be permitted to have that, I would stop complaining forever," said Sam. "You boys should thank your lucky stars. Me, I got to be satisfied with lining things up for others. Where does it get me?"

He was still talking to himself as Zena and Gilda dragged their companions out the door.

CHAPTER 3

"Va-va voom, as Gleason used to say! Have you ever seen such a swanky joint?" asked Morris, nudging his sidekick as they sauntered through the lobby of The Royal Palm.

"Only a good half of New York looked like this in the old days. Before they even built those towers and what a crying shame it was when the Arabs took them down but before they were up, the city was all glitter," said Mendel. "No, not since New York have I spun backward in time like this Palm sends me," said Mendel. "This isn't a minor leaguer, like Springfield," he added.

Art Deco in design, The Royal Palm was constructed with an eye toward one-upping Miami's most ostentatious hotels – The Deauville, The Doral, The Fountainbleu. The Palm's dozen swimming and wading pools were interconnected by a network of tiny tributaries. A diving pool, an eight lane racing pool, and a salt-water special comprised the luxurious auxiliary section. Smaller pools were perfect for kids.

The hotel buildings formed a right angle and most rooms looked out upon the swimming areas. Many guests had ocean views and virtually none found any structures blocking the light of the sky. Sumptuous suites included Jacuzzis, saunas, refrigerators, direct TV service, and a selection of videos and DVDs. For those wishing to combine work with play, computer ports with Internet access completed the package.

One large unit was cylindrical and all of its rooms granted exposure to pools and outdoor cafes. But Morris wanted nothing of it. "Since those 9/11 bombings, I will stay only on the second floor or lower. You can jump from two stories. Breaking my legs wouldn't be such a disaster. But, I don't want to go in flames."

"You're the one supposedly not concerned about the hereafter," said Mendel. "Drop the subject, at least for now, and let's please listen to these girls."

Zena was eager to show the M&M boys the courts. Gilda would have rather settled into their rooms but, as the little sister, she felt obliged to tag along.

"So, show us. What do the courts have, marble on top or something?" Mendel asked.

"Indoors and out. They have some down below on LL, and a dozen others as you walk to the beach. We can wait until tomorrow for a swim," said Zena.

"Costs a penny or two to play here, no?" asked Mendel.

"You got plenty, Mendel, enough to put us all up," answered Morris.

"Since I've known you, you've been no good. Who gave you the inside word on my finances?" asked Mendel.

"Boys, it's late and the day has lasted forever. Why not get over to Tessie's where we all stay? We need to settle," said Gilda.

"Just one moment, please," interjected Mendel. "For once, the oaf might have a point. For one night, I could foot the bill so our entire group could stay right here. What could it be, a couple hundred per room, no more, unless you're talking the overpriced suites?"

Neither woman responded. Zena took Gilda by the crook of the elbow and led her to a corner of the opulent hotel lobby. Innumerable palm trees, alive and fake, stationed in large circular pots, adorned the area. Spotting an individual twenty-five yards off was impossible due to palm blockage.

Morris waited until the girls left the premises and then, striding across the wide-angled room, poked Mendel and threatened a major wallop. "I was only kidding. But you, you got some nerve. What do you want, you think you're going to sleep with one of them? Where did you grow up, in some flophouse, a fleabag of a hotel in your big city, somewhere? I know enough, at least, to occasionally keep my mouth shut. Watch out for me. If I get mad enough, I'll strangle you," he hissed.

"Worth a try. When was the last time someone so sweet slept beside you, tell me why don't you? Five years ago or more, you can keep silent. Worried maybe you won't know what you're doing or worse, you know how but, so help you, cannot perform? There's always Viagra. Each day, it seems, you can get it cheaper, given the Internet and whatnot."

Morris did not respond and Mendel continued, "Don't get nervous. That's not what these dames are after."

Gilda and Zena soon returned. "Well, if you're asking, we could use one room with two double beds in it," said Gilda. "Should you boys agree, we would enjoy meeting you for breakfast at eight and a practice round a couple hours later. Mixed doubles begins Tuesday, the following day if you've lost count. I sometimes do," she said.

Morris lowered his chin toward his chest. "Since the debris came down on my friends, since the hoodlums took out the twin towers, I haven't been myself," he said. "Why have I worried so about death when fanatic people are after me? And here, we're talking, practically, about going on a double date. Go know, it's all right with me. I'll shlep along and put my old fashioned morals in my suitcase so nothing bothers me," he concluded. Speaking to himself, he continued, "They're geezer girls and still they want something to do with us? Whatever. I might as well keep playing the game."

Mendel took the lead, quickly negotiating for two choice rooms on the second floor. "Break my legs but not my brain," he would mutter as, once again, he cursed his lack of mobility. The accommodations offered views of both ocean and pool area. Mendel put the entire tab on one of his many credit cards. "No need to worry," he explained. "I could be dead by the time they bill me."

It was well past eleven that night before Morris and Mendel had settled in. Morris dispensed with washing up and left his clothes in his suitcase. Mendel, increasingly meticulous, especially when around women, insisted upon pampering himself before giving up and turning in.

Morris watched his friend putter about. "For once, could you please let a grown, overweight man sleep? And, what about you, forever complaining about aches and pains? Give it a rest."

Mendel said, "Can you imagine, we're a mere thirty yards or so away from two luscious women, our age no less? Do you know what that means, Morris?"

"I cannot guess and it means nothing. Yes, they were nice enough to invite us to play in this tournament. And you are completely out of your mind to think anything more? Turn off the light and be quiet, please," Morris barked. With that, the big man turned over and immediately began to snore.

When he awakened a few hours later to use the bathroom, Morris called for his friend. "Mendel, Mendel, I cannot find my nose even in this place. Where, dammit, is the bathroom light?" Silence. "Mendel, wake up, I need your help," and Morris went to his friend's bed and attempted to shake him. Morris, however, found nothing but blankets and sheets. The bedding was virtually untouched. Morris didn't know what to make of such a scene but, given Mendel's extracurricular doings as they motored south, Morris had a particular suspicion.

Morris relieved himself, washed, pressed hairs flat upon his head, and selected a dapper, color-coordinated outfit. He slowly walked from his own room number 206 directly down the hall to 214. Without pausing, he quickly rapped on the door. And a second time but still no answer. Once more with greater force. No response. Morris put his ear to the doorknob and imagined hearing the distinctive breathing of a deep sleeper. He turned, walked back down the corridor and, as if in a trance, continued while passing his own room until he reached the elevator.

Coffee, he convinced himself, would settle him. The elevator stopped, within seconds, at the mezzanine level. Morris intended to gorge himself on junk food which he visualized lodging like a water balloon in his ample belly. Preoccupied, Morris almost missed Mendel and Gilda before spotting the pair who sat side by side, platters of food surrounding them as she chatted and he chortled.

"There's my Moishkie," sang Mendel, as if his friend's arrival were pre-ordained. "Sit, it's after midnight, but we can still get you some food. Twenty-four hours no less, like the old days."

Morris felt his upper lip curl as sweat formed between his still dark, bushy brows. He never perspired normally. "I needed your help to find the bathroom and you weren't there," Morris bellowed, wishing he'd been drugged silly. "Here I am," he explained, in plaintive tones.

"So, take a load off. Gilda and I have been acquainting," said Mendel.

"An old but, in your case, tried and true routine," Morris responded, having regained his balance. "I'm sure this is simple, no?"

"Nothing more than what meets the eye," said Mendel. "Tell me, why can't two hungry people get a bite to eat?"

"Mr. Morris, there's nothing evil in what we've done," added Gilda. "We were simply famished. Besides, please be good and don't say a word to my sister. I worry what she might read into this."

It was Morris's turn to lighten. The big man celebrated positive times with a lift of his eyebrows. "I was just listening at your door. Sounds, to me, like she's sawing off quite a pile of wood up there. I wouldn't worry. I won't say anything to make you look bad. Only him. Do not be frightened that I am some kind of government spy. I'm sorry if that's the impression I'm giving, if that's what you think."

"What then, Morris?" asked Mendel

"I was worried, concerned about you," Morris responded, his forehead red and glistening.

"That is good of you but, my friend, we are quite fine here."

"So, I will leave." Mendel rose to block his way, but Morris shrugged him off and Mendel returned to the booth to reassure Gilda.

She sat silently, picking away at the burnt edges of an English muffin. Gilda started to get up, but Mendel motioned for her to sit.

"What's wrong?" he asked.

"I'm embarrassed. I don't think I should be here, never should have come here. Word is out, I know."

"Yes, he has seen us. But, I have smarts, too. Sit and be calm," instructed Mendel.

The next morning Morris awakened at sunrise, always the case, and found, to his delight, Mendel covered up to his chin with blankets and a quilt. Morris noisily bustled about, then spent fifteen minutes showering. He then emptied his entire suitcase before choosing an outfit for the day. He zippered the bag. Mendel began to stir; Morris smiled to himself.

"For Christ's sake, can't you let an old man sleep, you goy?" muttered Mendel, turning his face fully into his pillow. Morris saw that Mendel had not changed into pajamas. Mendel wore an undershirt and oversized boxer shorts. Morris didn't know what to think.

"All I've got to say is I'm glad you're back. I don't like it much in this place without you," he said.

"Keep it to yourself or people will think strange thoughts," whispered Mendel, trying to block out both light and sound.

"Why didn't you pick the skinny one?" asked Morris, trying to sound innocent.

"I took whoever was awake. Do you believe me? Must I come up with something better or does this satisfy you?"

"Let's drop it even if such talk makes no sense to me. If she's so enticing, what are you doing here? That's my real question."

"And my real answer is trying to sleep. Now, shut up."

Morris intentionally knocked over a flamingo figurine. He went to the bathroom and dropped a plastic cup onto the tile floor. He shouted, "Look, two, three hours from now we got to watch those dames play. Double time after that, I mean maybe eight hours from now we're going to be teamed with them, is that right? Shuffleboard practice, if I remember."

"Morris, if you went downstairs and got yourself maybe a danish, you would feel much better. Don't bother me. Goodnight to you," said Mendel.

Dozing off, Mendel heard Morris mutter, "I'm on my way."

Morris did not understand why he, so much larger in stature than his friend, was disproportionately timid. He was envious of the scrawny man's way with women and his bravado. Morris could not manufacture courage. He was a coward. But, he could bluster, put on a show when given a moment's notice.

Before seven the next morning, Morris began to prepare for the big event. He spent more time than necessary before the mirror, allowing himself a good fifteen minutes extra. Driving his body, despite its bulk, gave him strength. He ambled down the stairway, however awkwardly, to move the blood from his heart to his limbs. He wanted legs and wind, the endurance he enjoyed decades earlier. As a young man, Morris had played football each Sunday morning in a semi-pro league in Cleveland. The game moved from park to park. He remembered sprinting up and down stadium stairs forty years earlier.

An athlete prepares, he told himself time and again. It had been his mantra.

Now, once again, he would do the same. No, he would not overdo it but get those legs moving. Limber up. A little exercise would awaken his mind, sharpen his memory. He convinced himself that all of this was truth. "I can do this," he said aloud.

At first, he trotted along the corridor past the room where he knew the sisters were sleeping. Morris opened the fire door which led to concrete stairs. He began to descend, hitting each step, dreading an ankle sprain. He was panting hard but realized that deep breathing was a good thing. He felt the pulse in his veins. Someone had once told him to land on the balls of his feet. He feared, though, for those tiny bones protected by flimsy, inexpensive canvas tennis shoes.

He passed multiple landings and finally recognized the mezzanine where he knew the coffee shop, his domain, awaited him. One more door and Morris sniffed the familiar and alluring aroma of fresh cinnamon buns wafting into the hallway. He considered stopping to stuff himself but resisted. No, this would not become a moment in defeat. Morris simply turned and went back up the stairs. He was no quitter, and he would show Mendel and those girls. King Morris, he thought.

Up he went but his legs were rubbery and with every step he felt a bit more faint. Morris took steps two at a time but, nothing doing, he could not keep up the pace. Placing one foot in front of the next became an obsession. Approaching the second floor, he thought to pause but quickly rationalized that soon enough he would catch his second wind. Pain pierced his right side. This was a first for him – a runner's stitch, he thought. Such a stomach cramp he could outlast. The monstrous tentacles, however, would not relinquish such a vice-like grip.

Morris thought he might die and, surprisingly, this did not seem especially daunting. "Spike me, spear me, tear up my rib cage or what's left of it," he muttered. He paused to suck air. No luck. He would not give in, no coward he. His left arm was growing numb and the torture continued unabated. "Heart attack," he whispered. Morris wrapped his entire left side with his good right arm. He gulped and took a few steps upward. No relief. Maybe he would simply back down.

Not cave in, not cave in, that small voice inside him advised. He was amazed that not one person was using the staircase. Upward, once more, he turned. He began to count a beat for each step, hoping to take his mind off the misery. Walking slower and in rhythm, he began to believe that this might actually free his lungs. The sweat began to pour off him, at his hairline, then dripped beyond his eyes, creating soft, tiny pools on the steps beneath him. Suddenly, he felt embarrassed but also relieved to manage this journey alone. If this was a rite of passage to the next world, let him enter solo. Morris struggled to solidly plant both feet on the next concrete block. Straining to keep his head up, he felt his body drift away from him. He eyed the numeral four above him, tried to steady his vision. He grasped for the railing to the side with his good hand. "Let me survive," he said.

Then he fell. Attempting the approaching step, he missed the mark and tumbled. Reaching for the banister, he flew backwards, scraping his forehead, his palms, his forearms. He rolled heavily downward, stopping at last as he became wedged at a landing below. Soon, he lost consciousness.

Some time later, a young woman, illegally smuggling her poodle to her room, discovered the crumpled Morris all in a heap. For a few days now, the woman had come and gone by way of the staircase, successfully sneaking the dog out to her car through a basement exit. The old man before her lay inert, and she knew he needed help. But, she did not really wish to involve herself. Instead, she chose to rush back to her car with the pet. She hoped she would not look back.

Consumed with guilt, however, she went to the front desk. "There's a man dying," she announced. "He's fat and drooling all over himself," was all she could say. The morning clerk pressed a button to call an ambulance and left his desk to comfort the shaken woman. They took the service elevator to the third floor, and rambled to the end of the hallway, then up to the landing where the prone Morris, his face impassive, rested on cement.

"He's blue but he's breathing!" the clerk yelled. "Heart attack for sure! You can tell by the left side. Run downstairs for the ambulance. Tell them we got a live one but to move it. Then, get someone to find this man's family. Grab a body in the coffee shop for help. I'm gonna wait here with him."

"I think he's dead," said the young woman.

"Lady, dead he's not. Not yet. So, hurry, sister. Don't just stand there!"

She returned moments later with two attendants who carried a portable stretcher.

"Make way and let us at him," ordered a curly-haired man. He and his co-worker, whose veins bulged, hoisted Morris onto the portable cot.

Curly took charge. "Gang way, we're comin' through," he ordered, as if on a movie set. He and his co-worker, pallid and rail-thin, lifted Morris, as if he were a piece of furniture, onto the stretcher. There seemed no doubt that the fat man would immediately burst through the stretcher's canvas and injure himself further.

"You, Billy, under the middle. Hard to hold him up. You get the door," he said to the young woman, assisting. "Shovel him out of here pronto. Dunno how bad this is." Downstairs, a crowd had gathered around the ambulance. No one yet had tried to locate Morris's next of kin or closest friend. Instead, everyone gawked at the spectacle. The group instantly scurried Morris into the van. The skinny man began to work on him while Curly put the pedal to the floor. The young woman who had helped out returned to the lobby with the clerk.

"Who was that man?" asked the woman.

"Can't say. Forgot to ask. Too bad nobody thought to search his wallet."

"Well, you know that hospital. Call them," she told the clerk.

"That's the thing to do," he said, speaking loudly as if no one would hear him. "I hope he pulls through, makes a charmed recovery."

"Maybe we, maybe I overreacted. He might be okay, you know?"

Morris, fed oxygen at that very moment, revived...and complained. "Oy, what a pain, you cannot believe!"

"Don't talk, even in a whisper," implored the driver.

The other attendant, no longer oblivious, pushed forward. "Tell me where it hurts, exactly where, even press in on it."

Mendel rubbed his stomach, which rolled forward and took on a life of its own. Morris was sprawled on his left side.

"No higher?" questioned Curly.

"Yes, up a bit, but worse down on the middle of my big belly," said Morris, pointing at his mid-section.

The driver raised his eyebrows, shrugged his shoulders, and laughed heartily. The other man, supporting Morris, remained unemotional. His look was vacant.

The second, skinny man said, "Maybe it is not really an attack."

"What are you saying? That I got a heart attack? That I don't got, I mean have," said Morris.

"Don't talk," advised Curly.

Morris had lifted the oxygen mask off his face in order to speak. Now, he clamped it down again. The attendant forced it on. "That better?" Morris nodded his assent.

Within five minutes, they arrived at a hospital which Morris later described as "battleship gray and with that personality, too, if you want to know." Aware that he was being hustled into emergency, he saw doctors, nurses, and aides clustered, peering down at him. They poked and prodded, questioned him, and finally someone pronounced, "No, I don't think it's a full-fledged attack, but the heart is strained."

A doctor added, "Keep him for observation and we'll decide later how long. Get papers."

Morris continued to watch as people gradually began taking leave of the area, removing equipment as they departed. A nurse and doctor remained. "You've exercised your heart, Mr. (the physician glanced at a chart) Kahn." Morris thought exercise was a good thing, but he kept his mouth shut. "What were you doing on the stairway?"

"Exercising," he said, ever clever. "Getting ready for a shuffleboard match," Morris added.

The nurse and doctor looked at one another and Morris watched as their eyebrows rose in unison.

"Exercising?" asked the nurse.

"The doc's word. Running up and down the stairs."

"Well, is anyone with you where you're staying?"

Morris, straight-faced, replied, "Miss Zena Lewis, room 214. Not exactly with me, but you know," he said, winking with alternate eyes at each of the attendants.

It was just as well for Mendel, given Morris's absence, to dwell upon visiting Gilda. He rapped on the ladies' room door three times (a pre-arranged signal) and out she popped. Looking youthful and resplendent in matching lavender blouse, culottes, and skirt, Gilda slipped quietly out the door and closed it with a deft and steady hand.

"You mean she's not up?" questioned Mendel.

"Shush! She's a very heavy sleeper, but I don't want to even mention it," whispered Gilda. "We cannot chance anything. She sleeps past eight."

"What does she take, drugs? How else could she do it?" asked Mendel.

"Trade secret we share. Zena carries a flask of bourbon with her wherever she goes."

"Jews don't drink bourbon. But, if it works for her, that's the main thing," he said as Gilda nodded. Mendel brushed up against her shoulder while guiding her into the large elevator. She seemed willing enough to follow, a positive sign.

He led her downstairs to the main dining room, often and better used for banquets. He helped Gilda sit, then made haste for the men's room. Really, though, Mendel wanted a moment to examine his billfold, correctly anticipating that he was low on cash. He carried a number of credit cards but could not recall his balance. He always played it close. So, he stuck his Diner's Card in front on his wallet to have it handy. This was not the time to search down an ATM, although he had seen one, but where? Mendel splashed water on his hands and face before returning to the table. It was only when he sat that he realized he should have made use of the rest room.

Gilda was chatting, quite amiably, with the hunk of a young waiter before her. Mendel watched her watching him. Mendel ordered bacon and eggs. This was once a ritual for him during those many decades when he had lunch or brunch at restaurants maybe four or five times per week. Gilda politely requested two poached eggs ("one minute for each, please") and light white toast. "And a spit of champagne, too," called Mendel, before that impulse vanished.

"Would you believe he's Jewish?" asked Gilda, gesturing toward the muscle-bound waiter as she spoke to Mendel.

"I believe that. But, are you?" he asked Gilda, hoping to gain her complete attention for a moment.

"Well, what did you expect, someone with Spanish roots or something?"

"I did not know for certain. Forgive me for being stupid." Mendel blew his nose and it honked, as ever, causing him embarrassment. Then, he bowed to her.

The two of them stayed on for an hour or so, devouring a breakfast including fruit, Danish, and coffee. They spoke only of the immediate – food, shuffleboard partners, climate – and nothing of individual past or speculation of the future.

Mendel stood. "I'm stuffed, like a one-legged duck," he said.

"You don't look like one. You are one skimpy bag of bones," said Gilda, stretching, from her seat, for her sweater.

"Being trim keeps me alert," said Mendel, without a trace of hypochondria. "Not svelte but not fat." This time, he ushered her, by the arm, out of the room and pointed at the shuffleboard courts and the ocean beyond.

"Oh my God," said Gilda, "It's ten and I'm supposed to be on the practice court with Zena. She's probably fast asleep upstairs." Gilda turned toward the elevator.

"Easy," said Mendel. "They will, no doubt, give you fifteen extra minutes to prepare. I'll take care of it, just in case."

Mendel, in his youth, had been quite the enchanter. Son of an old world salesman who made money peddling imported trinkets on the Lower East Side, Mendel had long ago honed his way with words. His knowledge of women was intuitive. So he thought, so he said.

Only recently had he grown ornery and crotchety. He was certain that he could control those moods. When the proper and, in this case, still shapely muse beckoned, he summoned that seemingly forgotten but coolly infectious personality. Mendel retrieved the better part of his adolescence. Gilda left and he walked to the shuffleboard courts, having persuaded himself that the tournament committee would grant the Lewis sisters however long they needed, maybe half an hour or more, to practice.

Mendel fiddled with Gilda's cue, which she had presented to him as she walked off. He shot the disks forward with confidence, landing three straight within the lines. A few onlookers clapped and Mendel raised one eyebrow in acknowledgment. "Me and my buddy are joining some ladies in tomorrow's mixed doubles. I'm no novice now, so hold your applause until later." Mendel, suddenly limber, continued to shoot with Gilda and Zena's opponents, wowing them with his accuracy. He felt supple, free of encroaching aches and pains. He hopped on one leg, called his shot, and gloated as he settled one snuggly in the ten point triangle.

Gilda hustled in from the hotel, panting heavily, talking to herself. "She is not there. Neither is your friend Morris. I knocked on all the rooms. Where is he?"

"Without question, eating. He and I, we had one of our many, many disputes, and I told him to stuff his face. This was long before you and I went to the dining room."

Just then a message cackled across the antiquated speaker system. "Mr. Mendel Greenbaum, front desk, immediately. This means now!"

"Some wise guy," said Mendel. "Still, I should investigate," and attempted to rise quickly but, in the process, turned his ankle while turning to pivot.

"I suppose I should wait here," said Gilda, to no one in particular.

Mendel was back in five minutes. "Morris is in the hospital," he yelled to Gilda as soon as she was within earshot. "Zena is with him. We both got to go. He pushed Gilda forward, realizing that it was a first touch. She dropped her cue and walked quickly. As they moved back through the hotel lobby toward the cabby stand, he explained further, "Evidently, he strained the area around the heart but, thank God if there is one, it was not an attack. That's at least what they told me. He called for Zena from the hospital."

"And why my sister?"

"You don't know him, how to deal with him. This is practically a goy. A contradiction, though, you might say, since he is deeply religious. But not as in organized. No, instead, he has dabbled with no higher being, nothing spiritual. Don't ask me. But, maybe he has something." Mendel knew he was rambling but couldn't stop. "After all, at our age, we think of what might or might not be waiting for us. Those towers fell and, so help me, sometimes I am one hundred percent positive that checking out fast would be easier. Over and done with. More often, he thought, 'Why not continue? What are a few aches and pains?' Him, you go figure. For all the time we spend together, he doesn't talk much to me. Anyway, I spoke with Zena and the nurse at the hospital. So, let's go." With that, they boarded the cab which had just pulled up. Five minutes later they arrived at the hospital.

Morris gave up the ruse the moment Mendel entered the room. "It's good to see you, Mendel," he said, sitting up in bed. "I'm all right, just fine now. Nothing more than a pulled muscle which we get nearly every day, no?"

"Except you, you oversized sardine, now have a damaged ticker," Mendel said, wishing, instantly, that he hadn't blurted it out.

"They, these no-goodniks, they are holding me in captivity, for observation. Either I convince them that I should go or you'll sign papers and get me out."

"They're having a lot of trouble holding him down, even in bed," offered Zena.

"This one's some help," said Morris, reaching out to poke Mendel, who had to dodge the playful punch.

"Why didn't you call me earlier, you stinker?" asked Mendel.

"It's nearly beyond me to keep up with you. I'm not careful, you leave me in the dust. I wanted some female companionship, so sue me. Suppose, for example, I was actually sick," he said, winking at Zena. "Now, get me to the Royal Palm!," he roared at Mendel. "Get me out of this zoo they call a hospital. Have you ever in your life smelled such a putrid odor? A combination of old fish and one big Mr. Clean plastic, that's if you ask me."

"Already, he's back to himself," said Mendel.

Morris argued that he needed to be released, claiming that time was flying ever faster and he hadn't much air to use it up. He could not understand why indigestion or rib cage strain was thought to be serious.

"Look, so I overdid it. That much I admit. Why you have to make a federal case over it – this I cannot, for the life of me, understand."

The head nurse, waving her arms at once in an effort to be authoritarian, said, "Your doctor says you will be here for three full days, maybe longer. He wants tests run before you're dismissed."

Morris mumbled that he feared, above all, missing out on the doubles match. The team would forfeit the following morning. Morris became preoccupied with images: Mendel and Gilda fooling around on the court while he, Morris, was cooped up in the hospital; worse yet, he saw Zena watching the other pair....then Mendel in full regalia while he, the grand Morris, lay withering, first here, then in what was called a hospice. He could not imagine....once again, he smacked the hospital bed, enraging himself further. He cleared his throat and coughed....but no one seemed to pay him any mind.

Mendel, his body following his mind, soon found his way to the shuffleboard court. He wished Morris were there – to needle and nag him. Without the sarcastic big guy behind him, Mendel could not attack on the court. His game suffered immeasurably. Even in practice, he either undershot or pushed nearly every disk to the far right. Constantly citing his arthritic shoulder as he rubbed his elbow, Mendel alienated Zena. Gilda, though, took in the proceedings, cracked her knuckles just loudly enough and stifled her laughter by glancing down and away. She knew, at her age, that playing, simply playing the game was all that mattered.

CHAPTER 4

Morris moaned, grimaced and complained to anyone who would listen but acquiesced in the end, staying at the hospital for two full weeks. "I simply need a couple of hours, maybe each day to catch my breath," he explained, disgusted that his words fell flatly to the floor.

Finally, he was given clearance to return to the hotel. To celebrate, Mendel arranged for a dinner, complete with Zena and Gilda. Morris knew he had to raise the issue of expense. This was too much and he, even they, could not afford this forever. The women exchanged worried looks while Mendel remained composed.

"I, Mendel Greenbaum, will pick up the tab. No need to worry or fret, not even you," he said, winking, smiling, waving toward Morris. Mendel held his audience within the crook of his suddenly animated arm. He had transferred funds from checking to savings. Mendel pushed his chest just a bit forward.

A few days later, Morris whisked Zena out on a date. Off they went to the Municipal Auditorium. Billy Crystal and Robin Williams were in town for just one show in Miami. The M&M boys agreed that the comedians were nothing if not kids. Still, Morris was not about to miss this, and he did not want to go alone. The evening was a smashing success but Morris paid for it. His body needed rest, he did not have his usual pizzazz. By the time they arrived back at the hotel, well past midnight, he was bushed.

Short of breath, gasping and wheezing, he held to the wall as Zena helped him to his room. She held him fast, would not relinquish her grip until he was safely in bed. Finally, she moved off down the hall only to open the door handle, flip on the light switch, and discover Mendel and Gilda snuggled up, naked in bed, together. Neither of them stirred and Zena, baffled, could not figure. She ran down the hall, roused Morris who, upon hearing such upsetting news, responded with renewed vigor. He managed to maneuver his way up from the bed and half-limped, half-galloped back down the corridor, following Zena.

Morris coughed at the sight of Mendel, nude at least from the chest up, leaning his head upon the snoring Gilda. Zena barely had time to shove Morris into the hallway before he let loose with an enormous wail, "Little weasel, shlump! He's got some nerve claiming he's the one falling apart. What does he think he's sixteen, seventeen years old? It sickens me," he concluded swatting at but missing a hallway mirror.

Zena led him back down the hall to his room, insisting that he follow. Morris walked toward her, without questioning, relieved to be out of Mendel's proximity.

"You know, Mo, you just might take a tip from Mendel once in a while," said Zena.

"Your meaning?"

She cleared her throat. "That you, Mendel, Gilda, me, we're never too old to have those desires. This began, for me, what, about sixty years ago."

"So, we should follow suit or something? Have you no pride? Me, I'm no chicken here. At my age I'm sex-starved or something?"

Zena squirmed. "Sex is for all time, Mo. We're probably like some animals, like old goats, who want to go at it, horns and all. Admit it."

"I might agree with you. But, Mendel embarrasses himself and me, too, since I am his friend. Has he no shame?"

Zena avoided that question and, instead, asked, "Well, where do you propose to spend the night then?"

"In my bed, in my room."

"Listen, Mo, I was as surprised as you were. But, after all, is it so wrong? I mean, are they hurting one another? For people our age, love lives in memories. To seek a little human affection is not a felony. And, if sex was involved, so much the better. It's a new world, Mo. You can be called for departure any moment. Crazies crash airplanes into skyscrapers. You gotta get what you can when you can," she concluded.

"Zena, I tend to agree with you, even if I am shocked that you are so blunt, so outspoken. How you cannot feel ashamed is beyond me. A gorgeous woman like you."

"I want someone to touch me. It's been years since my last time. How about you?"

"Long enough. But, I'm not myself, not ready for full throttle." He clutched at his chest. "The heart strain, whatever, takes its toll. My wind isn't what it was."

"No need for us to pretend we're kids," she said. "What if we slept side by side? No touching, even. That could not possibly be so terrible."

"True. This is sudden, no? I am not prepared."

"What, you're worried about birth control? Come on, there isn't any sense."

"All right, you've convinced me. Besides, I keep telling Mendel to live only for today, like in that teenaged rock and roll music he loves so much. You've heard 'No Day Like Today'? How can I refuse?"

So, it was done. Mendel and Gilda remained in place while Morris and Zena took the other room. Everyone seemed content with the arrangement, even if they met as a quartet only for occasional meals. Saturday dinners were designated as a time for serious conversation.

"So, Mr. Big Shot, what is it that you've decided to do?" asked Mendel, picking at the half order of Veal Francaise before him. "You've got some secret up that sleeve and I want to hear it."

> "Mendel, put a cap on it," said Gilda, wiping her hand across her mouth.

Morris half rose, as if to address a throng at an installation if not at a roast. Then, he sat back down. Clearing his throat repeatedly, he boomed, "The truth is that Zena and I have decided to play some tournaments down here. I have been slowly regaining my strength and we have instituted a practice regimen. I would call us formidable." He stopped to crack a huge lobster claw with one hand. "Excuse me," said Morris, dripping melted butter as he slipped a wad of meat into the small clear cup. "We are about to float along, here in sunny, friendly Florida."

"Measly crumb, you little nothing," mumbled Mendel, catching a glimpse of his friend out of the corner of his eye. Mendel twisted his napkin until it began to shred.

"What about you two, Gilda?" asked Zena.

Mendel interjected, "We have decided to drive to Long Island, where I happen to own a home which has waterfront footage. Not only that, mind you, but a peppy little motor boat, too. If things continue to go well, perhaps we will settle there for good. If not, it's a big country, not so free as they say, but we'll find something."

"You have big plans, you, you mouse! Not rushing things one bit? And who's going to drive all that way, where do you get a car?" Morris shouted.

"You never heard of a rental? And I can drive," answered Mendel, pleased with himself since, he assumed, the question had been anticipated.

"I have a license, too," added Gilda.

"You haven't driven on a highway in years, Gilda," said Zena. "Going back and forth to the Food Bag is different than a car ride up and down, all around the entire east coast. Besides, you can't go off with him -- that is completely insane. What about our house in Miami?"

"Zena, this might be my final chance. I'll manage. The house you and Morris can have with my blessings, for now."

Everyone shifted uncomfortably since this was dangerous territory. A discussion of lifestyle, change of ritual, new habits to form...and what if someone's prospects were dwindling? This was taboo. This generation thought itself the first to care for elderly, slow-to-expire parents. Nobody wanted to look squarely in the mirror. Plastic surgery, such as Botox? Such a procedure was not yet routine. Wrinkles and creases told it all -- where you had been, what might yet occur. The map of one's face revealed a life's chapters.

After a short while, Morris broke the spell. "You simply cannot leave us, without letting me know where and how to reach you. Besides, this plan of yours," he said, wafting the air, "is trite and just so much foolishness."

"You never heard of a phone? Or computers, email and whatnot. We'll be in Clearview and the directories, if they allow it, will include both of our names." Mendel pointed at Gilda, cinching any doubt that she was a verifiable accomplice.

"Your mind is made up, what can I say?" asked Morris.

"Well then," said Mendel, having for once shut down the larger man. "Now that it's out, I am not ashamed to confess being embarrassed. I did not plan on divulging so much so soon."

"Nonsense!" thundered Morris. "This is reason to celebrate. We're alive, that much is for sure. Whoever said old age wasn't worth a million bucks....these days, even more? Waiter, come over here," he implored. "Let's live!" bellowed Morris for all to hear. Everyone in the room turned to listen. Morris was oblivious. Then, he realized. "Sorry," he said, in a softer tone. "Champagne all around. We're rejoicing here," he explained to the waiter.

Suddenly, Zena and Gilda went off by themselves but only as far as a vacant table to get some privacy.

This did not please Mendel. "You would think that they could stay with us through the meal, without interruption. If you ask me, it's rude to leave the table. That's what I was taught."

"Times change, people don't," said Morris. "Some smart man or woman said that and it counts right here and now. Well, maybe not. You know, Mendel, it's a damn shame we didn't meet them ten years ago."

"To be honest, and I hope my wife, Hester, she should never hear me from her grave, I wish I met Gilda long ago. Forgive me."

"I happen to feel the same way, Mendel," said Morris. "Even if it makes me guilty before God to say so."

"Your Ruthie and my Hester, they should both be happier now without us but these new women, these Lewis sisters, why did it take until now?"

"They are a couple of wild cards, I agree," added Morris. "Look, they're coming back."

"Thanks to god for that. Morris, just one thing more: what if I lose you? What if this thing doesn't work out and then you're the first to go. What then?"

"Please, Mendel, don't be foolish or sappy." And with that, Morris smacked his friend in the back, twice and then again. "For good measure and luck with our health!"

As the women reappeared, Mendel lifted his cup of coffee. "Ladies, and one oversized gentleman beside me, let us drink to all of our futures. Our youth may be forgotten but still you must go for it, enjoy the moment. To hell with the next world, let's celebrate for now!"

***

Everyone went separate ways the following morning.

"Mendel, I need to get some things out of the Flamingo house," Gilda said. "Zena and I store dresses there even though we most often live in Miami when we're down here. It makes us feel younger to be in touch with Mildred. Her finger points forward. You saw her. Anyone can tell that she's got a couple things going for her. We will all be goners but she'll be steaming like a locomotive."

"Nonsense. Why even think that way, letting it enter your mind? First order of business, we need a car. I want to be on the road," Mendel said, with impatience.

Mendel, unlike Morris, did not wear bravado naturally. Poised in the hotel lobby, he tried, acting against type, to amplify his presence. Hailing a cab successfully, Mendel intentionally talked down to the taxi driver. "We need you to speed, got that, to the nearest car rental joint. Got that?"

"Hertz, Avis, or a no-name?" asked the driver.

"The fanciest, most luxurious, the best, my good man," said Mendel. He then shifted to whisper in Gilda's ear, "Not an intellect, that Joe."

The driver, hearing the put down, made a beeline to the nearby Hertz agency where he deposited the couple.

"Wait here," instructed Mendel and off he went, limping into the agency. Fifteen minutes later he returned, stomping forward in full stride, his face flushed, and his hair disheveled.

"What's wrong?" asked Gilda.

"They got no Mercedes, no Jaguars."

"Mendel, this is a regular car rental place and why would you want a German car anyway?"

"I don't think about German, only top of the line. It's just the best. Maybe Jaguar can match. We want top-notch. I got the money, why wait? After those towers came down, just like the walls or columns, I can't remember which, in Jericho, you must live each day. Now, this is even more vital. So, spend your money, that's what I tell myself. That's why."

"Where do you have us going, Mendel?"

"You and me, we are going five blocks up to the Mercedes dealer. Maybe we'll have better luck there. Nothing but the best for us, Gilda. I've heard you can lease top models."

"Mendel, you don't have to buy a product that Nazis built."

"Will you listen to the lady? I want a top-notch machine. She's worried that it somehow means something other than Mercedes Automatic. Come on and follow me into the showroom," he said. "There she sits, I can see the sign. What do you think?"

She nodded. Mendel escorted her to a soft chair in the showroom. He looked at a few cars, ambled into an open office with a salesman. Just a few minutes later Mendel emerged, a grin spreading across his face.

"Gilda, the man is a consummate con. Somehow, he's convinced me that renting is a waste of time. I'm buying. Which color do you like?"

"Deep blue, night time blue, Mendel. But this is crazy, this notion. Who knows if either of us can drive? Together, maybe we're one solid driver."

He pinched both of her cheeks. Mendel turned to the salesman and said, "We'll take that one. Make me your best deal and I shall remember you until they lower me into my grave."

"By all means, sir."

"It doesn't include a standard shift, does it?"

"Many cars do."

"Then, we need another car. Automatic, I said."

Well, there are two or three out behind."

"The silver convertible or the bright yellow sports coupe. Show me those," ordered Mendel. He turned to Gilda. "Let's see if we can squeeze into one of those babies," he said. "Assuming we get in, we'll never, the two of us, get out. Look at that canary bird color on that one, will you?"

Mendel asked his auto sales friend, his latest pal, to draw up papers on the yellow car, complete with a sunroof. It took longer than expected to shine the vehicle, authorize Mendel's personal check, and attach a temporary license plate. The company, with a sale in the works, eagerly took on the challenge, red tape and all. Someone instantly appeared with doughnuts and drinks. Less than one hour later, Mendel and his girl, Gilda, were ready for action.

They managed just a few hundred miles the first night, driving up the coast in Florida. Gilda sat nervously, deep-set eyes glued to the road, hands twitching in her lap. Mendel repeatedly wiped his brow, even if this was needless. The powerful air conditioning nullified oppressive heat and humidity. Every so often, Mendel snapped off the air and opened his window. He thought the tropical air might awaken him. Finally, Mendel pulled the Mercedes into a motel parking lot just outside of Vero Beach. A former Howard Johnson's, it was now called Breezy Way. His imagination on the loose, Mendel struggled to manipulate his stiffened body out of his seat.

"So, canary bird, here we are off the mark. I know we haven't gone that far, but at least we're off. Tomorrow, we step up the pace."

"A dive like this you're taking me to? Of all the places in Florida, Mendel, this is the best we can do? What, a twelve room motel in the middle of nowhere?"

"You want to drive further, be my guest. I, for one, cannot see straight," he answered.

"I don't drive on a regular basis, almost never at night, unless it's an emergency. Zena is the night owl. Tomorrow, as I have told you, I will drive. Give me time. I suppose it's just as well that you stopped. But here?"

"Unless I am severely mistaken this might be the place the old Dodgers stayed in – Dodger Inn, if you know what I mean. The old goats, unless I am completely nuts, still occupy this place during spring training. Or did the Brooklyns move to Arizona? My mind is so fuzzy now I can't remember. Well, this is where they once were."

"If they stayed in this dump, they must have been totally crazy. And even I know that it's the Los Angeles Dodgers now," said Gilda, patting him gently on the head.

"Thank you for the update, as they say. Now, let's get registered and settled in." And so, as Mr. and Mrs. Mendel Greenbaum, they snagged warmed-over burgers and fries in what passed for the motel restaurant, and dragged themselves, the food, and their luggage into their tiny room.

"You think they could find a flea-bitten bed worse than this one if they tried? What is this?" yelled Mendel, as he collapsed on the baggy mattress, which poked at his bottom.

"Look who's complaining. If it's good enough for your beloved Dodgers, it will do for us. Besides, we'll be that much closer….," Gilda said.

"Don't go embarrassing me so much so soon."

"What, you think someone else is listening? So what if they are. We're not so young and who cares anyway?"

"Gilda, come now," said Mendel.

"Mendel, shmendel, relax. You would think you never once touched a woman."

"I touched you all last week."

"I mean before that."

"Except for one time, it had been years," he said.

"For me, too, I have to make that confession."

"It's been years since you touched a woman. This is news that I hope is true," said Mendel and they both laughed.

"Gilda, I want to tell you something so sit next to me." He positioned himself next to her on the edge of the undersized bed. Mendel held one of her hands loosely within both of his. "Gilda, I don't know if I can sleep with a woman anymore."

She laughed softly. "You fell asleep next to me all last week, Mendel."

"No, I might not be able to make love like I used to is what I mean." He paused. "You see, when a man gets to be my age, he can lose what, a way to get himself excited or something."

"Mendel, I am too old and I don't want babies."

"I'm serious so don't fool. I can't have an erection is what I am trying to say," said Mendel, letting go of Gilda's hand as he stared directly at his own shoes.

"So what, for one thing. And, for another, if it concerns you so, there's Viagra and more from what I hear."

"And if I cannot perform, you end up sleeping with a wet, soft noodle. You like to cuddle up to that, fine. But, I can't imagine it's all that much fun."

"Mendel, I will tell you that I'm through with spears and snakes, whatever it is you're thinking. If that was on my mind, I would not be here this very moment. Give me some credit. What, was I born yesterday?"

"So, this news of mine does not disappoint you?"

"However big or small and the rest. That does not impress me, not now for certain."

"Okay. Enough. Soon this talk will embarrass me," he advised.

"Mendel, how old are you?" Gilda asked.

"Old enough and older than you."

"No, you're just a boychik. Chutzpa on the outside, you got plenty. Inside, you act like a little boy." She put her arm around his rickety frame and hugged him to her. Mendel, in response, showed his crooked teeth. Then, they slept.

Stomach cramps kept Mendel awake more often than not that evening. He was up for good before six, and his breath felt stale. Gilda was snoring peacefully and Mendel thought that, rather than risk disturbing here, he would slip over to the restaurant for a quick breakfast. Maybe food would fuel his day. The greasy meal the night before must have done him in. He burped loud enough to jar Gilda. Mendel exhaled fully only when she settled back on her pillow. She propped it up, with her hands, from underneath.

Mendel saw the Breakfast Special sign in the window: Eggs, bacon, toast, home fries, coffee -- $3. Mendel summoned the waitress. He could not take a pass on such a cheap meal. "Gimme the special," he commanded, and then perched himself upon a bar stool at the end of a long counter.

The waitress sidled over and bent forward, affording Mendel a long view of her, including a look down her shirt. "It takes a while to cook the bacon. You got a few minutes?" she asked.

Mendel considered. He always thought he had time on his hands. Now, moments, minutes, hours, days, weeks, months, not to mention years were a scarce commodity. He looked at the waitress, who continued to tilt her torso, and said, "Plenty of time for the right person." Mendel noticed a distinguished looking man, whom he felt he knew but from what circumstance he could not recall, eyeing him from the other end of the long bar. The man had a notebook with him and seemed to be reporting. He looked at Mendel, then at the page. Mendel stared at him while cursing, beneath his breath, his own sub par vision.

Mendel, preoccupied, hadn't any idea that twenty minutes had passed by from the moment he ordered until the time of delivery. "Quickly," he mumbled to the waitress as she set down his plate before him.

"Excuse me?"

"I said excellent service."

She laughed. "Sure, buddy." The waitress shook her head and wiggled her bottom at Mendel as she strolled back toward the kitchen.

He speared a larger than average home fry with his fork and inched the potato toward his mouth. Mendel suddenly realized who the man was but could not believe it to be true. After all, spring training had concluded months before. What was he doing here now? Besides, he must work for a living and whatever he did down here wasn't work. Sure, Mendel had read that the man joined the Dodgers during spring training and helped to develop young guys into accomplished batters. It did not, however, appear that the ballplayers were currently in town.

What's more, a clear and expanding bald spot, the size of a silver dollar, drew attention to the back portion of the handsome man's head. Well, what was so unusual? Mendel, on the other side of eighty, was nearly hairless. This guy, a bit younger, could have lost a little hair, too. After all….

Mendel took his plate and silverware in one hand, carried his half-filled coffee cup in the other, and moved down the counter until he was corner-to-corner with the stranger. He sat down, intentionally rattling the Formica table top. Only then did the man look up.

"Pardon me," said Mendel, "but unless I am seriously mistaken, I believe that you are the erstwhile Duke of Flatbush, Duke Snider, before my aging eyes."

The man smiled warmly. "As a matter of fact, that would be me. What can I do for you?"

"I am just stunned," said Mendel. "You are The Silver Fox and I was such a fan you couldn't imagine. What are you doing here?"

"Keeping a low profile. Scouting, working for the Dodgers. Trying to be in touch with baseball. Looking at Class A ballplayers."

"Duke Snider," said Mendel dreamily. "My hero, even if we are something like the same age? Morris will kill himself for missing this meeting."

"Who?"

"No, nothing. A man I know, like the size of Don Newcomb. Listen, you were the best New York had to offer. I grew up in Sheepshead Bay after we moved away from Williamsburg. Don't let anyone fool you. You were better than Mantle and Mays, even put together. You had the grace. The toast of the entire city, you were in those days."

"When you knew me, I was not thinking of what was ahead – like all of us do now. Or, am I way off base? I always talk in the game's language. But, you followed me and hardball back then, did you?" asked Snider. "You still live in Brooklyn?"

"Close enough since I intend to go back to my place on Long Island. You know, since the disaster, I want to get back in touch with the city. Not most of my friends who could not care if they ever saw New York again. It's in my blood and, although I don't have many people left, they all came from New York. So, I am moving from Massachusetts. I am on vacation south of here in Florida. But, it's time to try to be somewhere important. For the duration if you can understand," said Mendel.

"Oh, I get your meaning. I miss New York sometimes, not always," said the Duke.

"I bet you don't miss the way those goddamned Mets treated you when you came back at the end of your career."

"Can't say it was fun. But, I had lost it by then. Most athletes have, even that Michael Jordan, who was not an exception. Listen, I've got to move on. I'm due at the ballpark at eight to hit fungoes to a kid outfielder they're watching. Need to shower first. It's still the pre-game ritual that remains with me."

"Sure, sure, Duke. Listen, could you just sign a napkin so that my friends actually believe this happened?"

With a flourish, Snider autographed the napkin.

"Thanks, Duke, and good luck to you."

"Same." Mendel watched the former slugger, still formidable if stooped, gather himself together as he left the restaurant.

Just then the waitress emerged. "Anything else? This okay?" Mendel didn't respond. She snapped her fingers twice, and crisply, before his eyes. "Buddy, you alright?"

"Oh, fine, thank you. I just talked with Duke Snider, who was always a prince in center field. The fifties – in the borough of Brooklyn? Capiche?"

She smiled. "You must mean Eddie. No, he's not Duke Snider, just a money-grubbing ringer. Others have made the mistake before you. He plays right along because this gets him excited if you know what I mean. He's got it all down pat, playing the part."

"You have to be kidding. He's not Duke?" said Mendel, dumbfounded.

"I don't want to hurt your feelings since he is an Ed and so is Snider. Don't get down in the dumps about it. If you want him to be Duke Snider, no one else will know. You have the napkin, right?"

"Are you suggesting that I pretend he really was Duke Snider, even now?"

"Hey, if it rattles your chain, if you want to impress someone, go for it. You got the Hancock, yes?"

"Well, for Eddie -- whoever he really is."

"No, for you and yours, this is the McCoy, the signature – the genuine article."

Mendel shrugged. "Maybe you got something. Okay, I will ante up." Mendel stood to pay. He took a ten dollar bill and pressed it to the waitress's palm. "You made the day for an old man."

"Nothing to it. Thanks," she said and sashayed away, swinging her hips.

Mendel strolled out of the restaurant and made his way back to his room. Gilda was up, showered, and packed. Mendel eagerly stuffed his clothes into a suitcase, then sat on it to fasten the latches. Gilda fetched pastries and coffee for the road and, within thirty minutes, they were off.

More than pleased to have the wheel to himself, Mendel watched and daydreamed, wondered about their life together. Who would have thought it? He had assumed that he would gradually wither away. When he died someone would discover his remains days after the event. Anyway, who would care? Now, suddenly as can be, life was so, so different. Mendel, his eyes attentively glued to the interstate, caught occasional glimpses of run-down houses. He felt his vision had improved. The print on road sign clarified. What did it matter that Mendel could not determine where they were bound? With Gilda, a woman he adored, sitting by him, he might live another fifteen even twenty years. He was convinced they were perfect travel companions. That much he knew and what could matter more?

By the third day, as they moved northward in Georgia, Gilda summoned the courage to drive. Mendel's instructions to his reluctant lady were brief and to the point: "With a beauty like this, you don't need anything more than point her straight and hold steady," he advised.

"You don't know me this way. I am terrified of machines. And this one, I grant you looks pretty, but I got something against it."

Mendel remained silent. He did not address the issue until days later as they approached Washington, D.C. He did much of the driving but Gilda took the wheel once again in Fredericksburg, Virginia. Mendel had taken them through North Carolina. He wanted his mind to wander. The forbidden woman, Lucy, was still on his mind and he could not lose her image. Here they were.

So, he began to sing show tunes from musicals he had seen decades earlier: "South Pacific," "Oklahoma," "Carousel," "Annie Get Your Gun." Mendel, as a much younger man, tried to get to Broadway as often as possible. He was taken by surprise that Gilda knew all the tunes. Not only that, she had performed in community theater groups for years. Mendel sang with passion while, despite himself, he thought of Lucy.

Gilda, at the wheel, cruised just below the speed limit, never exceeding sixty-five mph. She seemed familiar, even at ease, but, beneath it all, she stewed. Finally, she could no longer keep silent. "Mendel, this car is so much like those Germans: spotless, perfectly tuned, absolutely inhuman. You put in the key, turn on the engine, it drives itself. So fast, smooth, and precise. It could kill; they did."

"A Ford would have been better? Or a Chevy maybe? One of those junks would have fallen apart in Jacksonville and you would have been stuck with nothing. You want a car where you get your hands filled with grease every twenty-five miles? Gilda, what do you have against this Mercedes? Really, the war was over sixty years ago. There's good Germans and bad Germans. Just like Americans or even Jews. Look at Israel where they kill Palestinians and vice versa, for reasons geniuses create – so many explanations it seems they are like a pack of flies even. So, please be quiet. This car gets us where we want. Later, if you say so, I will sell it and get something else."

"My brother was killed in Cologne," she said.

Mendel stopped short and hugged her close. "Why didn't you tell me earlier? I am so sorry for what I said, for you."

"It was never for sure that a German killed him. What I know is that he went over there and did not come back. No one could fully determine exactly what happened. But, this was Hitler's war," she said.

"That I cannot dispute," said Mendel. "Because of that, though, you won't drive a car made by people who probably had nothing to do with any of that?"

"Mendel, that is the problem. Maybe they did not but maybe they did. Have you ever been to Germany?"

"Once, while on one of those group tours, we passed through but mostly traveled in Austria, France, and Switzerland. We did go down the Rhine. So?"

"You didn't feel strange, odd, even guilty being there? With Zena, I went to both Dachau and then to Munich, where she had some people. She wanted to remember more clearly. What I saw, sanitized as it was, I will never forget."

"What good would it do," implored Mendel, "to live your life in the past? I knew someone not well, but an acquaintance – I played with him shuffleboard and he worked in the Trade Center. What am I to do? Never go to New York. That would be insane. I feel a twinge when I go to the city, but I go. How can you stop living? This car could have been built by the most upstanding people you could ever meet. So, I shouldn't drive it?"

"What I am saying is that we can never forget our families, friends, our people. Lessons."

Mendel smacked his forehead. "Listen, drive the car to Washington and we'll see if we can keep arguing all the way there."

"That, at least the driving part, is what I am doing, in case you haven't noticed. It's just another twenty-five miles or so. Then what?"

"We play at being tourists, try to be carefree. None of this constant examination which gives me a splitting Excedrin headache. Just for one day we pretend we have no troubles. " He shrugged from beneath the harness which Gilda insisted he wear. Mendel had complained, to deaf ears, that it cut off his circulation, made his bad shoulder even worse.

Mendel, navigating, led them on a series of wrong turns, detouring well beyond The District and clear into Maryland. He was determined to highlight the tour with stops at the illustrious national landmarks:

the White House; the Lincoln and Jefferson Memorials; the Washington Monument. He hoped to avoid the Pentagon, a reminder of September eleventh. Mendel had always avoided discussions of mortality at any cost. Now more than ever. If he saw the building, Gilda would no doubt speak of the tragedy and he would be caught. Meanwhile, he had lost his bearings and, extended his arm across Gilda's body.

"What now, for God's sake, Mendel, what are you doing?"

"Let's lower the top so that I can see better," he said.

"Can't you wait until I stop the car? There are controls, latches. Sit back down," she said and put her hand out to block him, as if he were a small child.

"A mechanic, no less, I get hitched up with a mechanic."

"Your choice, if I am clear," she said.

"A wise one. So, can you pull over there, by the phone?"

"You got someone special to call, like the President, maybe? An old friend of yours?"

"Not the President, whom I did not vote for, but my boyhood neighbor Herbie and his wife. This is true, provided one or both of them are still alive. They were always begging me to visit. Even if we needed two rooms. You'll never guess where they live."

"Around the corner from the White House," she said.

"No, Gilda, in the Watergate."

"I should have known. Were your friends there when it happened?"

"I cannot say that I am sure but it's been, what, thirty years or so? Herbie has been here for I don't know how long. I lose track. But, we do email back and forth every so often."

"Politics I don't follow so closely," she said.

"Maybe I can get his number through information, do you think?"

"What's his last name?"

"Zwiebel, but I'm not sure if that's with ie or ei or bel or ble."

"With a name like Herbie Zwiebel you won't have a big problem, Mendel. There won't be more than one in the book."

Soon enough, Mendel called. The message he received informed him that "Frieda and Herbie were out to dinner, back soon, and would return all calls. So, please leave a number." Mendel was taken off-guard with the request and he hadn't a phone number to supply for a return call. "Why," he asked himself, "did I never take a deal and sign up for a cell phone?"

They drove around the city and made their way, eventually, to the Watergate. There they slept that night, in the Zwiebels' guest room which included, among other items, memorabilia Herbie had collected while overseas during the Second World War. He had managed to keep two swords, various medallions, helmets, and even a handful of brown shirts. While Mendel snored, Gilda, wide-eyed, thrashed about uncomfortably, so certain was she that vestiges and images of the Third Reich would forever haunt her.

At breakfast the next morning, before they left, she spoke up. "You'll have to pardon me, Herbie, but why the small museum of Nazi artifacts?"

"Good question but you may be disappointed to hear that this has simply been my hobby. Actually, we have a club, a group that trades, in this country, and in Europe, too. You know that gold dagger?" She nodded. "That one I got myself off a dead man when I was stationed in Germany. Lifted it out of his hands."

"Herbie's done more with this since he retired," Frieda explained. "He goes to conventions, as far away as the West Coast. I, myself, could do without. But, you know, this doesn't hurt anyone. Still, I tell him to keep the collection locked in a cabinet in the spare bedroom. Otherwise, that would be the end of it," she added.

"So, what do you think, Herbie, of this catch? She's some woman, and that is a fact," advised Mendel, nervous and hoping to shift the conversation. He gestured toward Gilda.

"This is what we used to call in the old days a knockout, drop-dead gorgeous, Mendel," said Herbie, trying to be sincere while his gaze betrayed his distraction. Forcing himself to concentrate, he stared intently over Mendel's shoulder as Mendel tried to sneak a peek at Frieda. "Where you headed next?" asked Herbie.

"Long Island, where I own a home. I rented it out last year, thinking I would sell. Luckily, I procrastinated because now (he winked) I know just what to do with it."

"Mendel, if you ask me and you didn't, it's not a simple piece of cake for men of our age to run a household. You're better off with a condo, a coop, a community. I can give you advice. I've tried them all."

"Well, I appreciate your thoughts on the matter, Herb, but the die has been cast or whatever that saying is. If it doesn't work out, we'll go to option b or c or maybe even more. But, I am not so decrepit as I look or as you imagine."

"You two always have a room here. Let me tell you something, in case you arrive and we're not here. For anyone in a pinch, we hide a key beneath the umbrella stand by the elevator down the hall. They never move the thing to vacuum. If you ever get stuck, snatch the key and let yourself in. Eat and drink. We go out a lot – probably if we're not here, we're at brunch or dinner."

The two old men simultaneously rose and hugged, as if this were a dance just remembered. Each recognized the possibility that he might never see the other again. The ladies made small talk while Mendel and Herbie dragged out the suitcases. Gilda slid in behind the wheel of the Mercedes. It was still early morning.

***

Zena, the single-minded one, grew more addicted than ever to shuffleboard. Purposefully persuading Morris to join her on the court time and again, she had him thinking that amateur tournaments were, despite distractions, both challenging and entertaining. Morris fought the impulse to sarcastically degrade the variety of aged and crippled types he saw dragging their sagging frames onto the courts.

Thanks to Zena, they stayed on for another couple of days at The Royal Palm. Mendel, who had felt guilty about leaving so abruptly, made fiscal arrangements in advance so that Morris and Zena would not have to worry. Mendel insisted that he pick up the tab on this one.

An edgy Morris appeared on the final morning of their stay. "So, where do you imagine we will live as we tour about playing your beloved shuffleboard?" he asked Zena.

"I suggest that you stay in bed and enjoy your last few moments of luxury. One thing I will not guarantee is comfort," advised Zena. And with that, Morris removed the pullover shirt he was about to tuck in.

He realized that the mid-summer scorcher of a sun, complete with poisonous rays, was no friend at this juncture in life. Instead, he would cuddle next to this woman, for whom he had developed a blinding, binding trust. Why not? Morris had learned to compromise. If she wasn't Elizabeth Taylor in her prime, neither was he Richard Burton nor even Sean Connery. So, he slid back in next to Zena, who smoothed his brow.

"You know, Mo, you could stand to lose a few pounds," she said. "A little diet would be a good thing."

"Diet, shmiet, I have looked this way since I can remember. The only thing is I'm not as strong as I once was. Give me a few weeks and that, too, will change."

"Those doctors at the hospital said your heart would work better if it weren't surrounded," she said, grabbing a soft wattle of flesh at his chest.

"I'm not one to dispute. But, I look like this. This is me," he said. "Besides, I wouldn't call you a lightweight by any stretch," he said, patting her soft, rounded rear he so adored. "Don't get me wrong. It's not that I object," he said.

She smiled. "Most of my weight comes with age. Don't you know women change into pears after fifty? Anyway, I wouldn't mind taking off some. Maybe we could do this together."

He raised both eyebrows and wiggled one, a trick he had mastered as a young teenager. "Not yet. Let's have breakfast up here today, one last cholesterol kick," said Morris.

That they did.

Afterward, they enjoyed intimate moments -- courtesy of Mendel. Within a few days, they had assumed rental payments on someone else's condo in North Lauderdale. It was easy to find sublet connections in Florida, as a collection of snowbirds flew north during the summer months. Mildred Flamingo, in this case, was key. She knew a couple who had gone off to visit children and grandchildren out west. They had asked her to find "responsible adults" to live in their house during their absence. Money meant little so the rate was reduced. Zena jumped at the opportunity, hoping for a home base. She so wished to pursue her shuffleboard career. Morris had another agenda, thinking that, in later life, it would be fine to once again marry. Nothing to lose, he reasoned. Still, Morris wondered whether Zena was the real thing.

Two days after they had settled in, she informed him of her plans. "Mo, I've entered us in a mixed competition at Sunrise Lakes next week, then at Castle Gardens several days later."

"I'm glad you asked me first," said Morris. "I'm no Floridian and this business of condominium hopping I don't know about. You got to consult first with Gilda," he said.

"I forgot they don't have any condos in Cleveland," she answered.

"Not so much that. I was never one to mingle. Chatting all day long is not a great thing for a person with the attention span of a gnat. When I was a working man, that was my life. I cannot see playing shuffleboard all of the time."

"So, what did you do? Somehow, we never discussed that."

"Some selling. I helped my uncle run a hotel once upon a time, long ago. Most often, I was a commercial artist."

"You?"

"I painted signs. Huge billboards all over Ohio. Every detail had to be perfect before I put aside a project. After years of it, I realized that I would be the only one to notice if I made a mistake. So, I worked faster, made more money," he said. "Never enough to satisfy me."

"Mo, what does this have to do with not wanting to play shuffleboard tournaments now?"

"Well, only with passion can I possibly do something all of the time. I like fooling with disks and sticks, but something's missing. Can't put my index finger on it, Zena."

Silent, her thought process elsewhere, she looked away.

Nevertheless, Morris played two tournaments before insisting that he and Zena have a serious conversation before he found himself committed to other events. The following weekend, having done nothing more than eat, swim, play a few more rounds, and sleep, Morris called for Zena's attention.

"Zena, this is all just hunky-dory, but not for me, at least not on a permanent basis. I want to go back North."

"And what about me, Mo?"

"With me. Come back to Springfield with me."

"What do I know of that town? What would I do in godforsaken Springfield, Mass? This could be the worst move I ever made."

"For one thing, it would surprise you just how many people you find in our age bracket. You must think old people live only down here. A myth, Zena. We could play in tournaments there, live in my house. I won't have to sell and, besides, I never wanted to. They told me over and over it only made sense. Now, nonsense."

"Morris, what do I need another house for, at this point? I'll give you a house. We've got enough to worry about right here. I don't want responsibility, especially since, as you put it, this is your house. I would rather spend my time doing better things."

"Such as?"

"Shuffleboard. The truth is, I might consider such a move, but if only I could stay away from my pain-in-the-neck sister a bit longer and, you promise you can find me a job. Third – after a year, I would want to see my sister," she said.

"What's the big magilla, woman? You're easy to please."

"I am still the little sister, Mo. Gilda, forever, she will check on me. She's protective and she will never, ever leave. If we go, she will do her best to be a fixture in that town. She will be there, somehow, weekend after weekend."

"Mendel will stay on Long Island. Of this, I am sure. I have bigger plans for us. Including marriage."

"Never have I married, Mo. It's different, at this point, for me. Yes, I always wanted to. Gilda and me, they call us spinsters. When we were young, we each had our share of men, wine, romance…. That was fifty years ago, more even. A wedding is not in my plans. I'm sorry to disappoint you."

"You intend to live this way forever?" he asked.

"I, for one, do not speak of the future. For now, this is good."

"I see. I have been in this mosquito-bitten Florida for more than a month now. Wouldn't you care to try a climate where your clothes are not soaked with sweat in five minutes? Not to mention bugs, salamanders, red ants, and, without doubt, the residents."

"Morris, I am willing to try but I would be lying if I told you this would be a permanent move for me. I've never been there and I will not lock in."

"We'll fly. No matter this hyped-up crazy security and search lines. Not a problem. I'm not about to drive fifteen hundred miles ever again."

"On that we agree. I sleep and read on airplanes. And, if we bring a picnic, I will eat, too."

Within a week, they were gone.

CHAPTER 5

"So, this is your palace, the home of your dreams, and that, across the street, is Forest Park. You say this Olmsted was the master, no? Now, I know why you were bending my ear for three straight days," said Zena.

"You claim you know something about parks. This one cannot be topped," said Morris. "Look at those maples, and the cluster of pine. Dogwoods galore. Bushes so sculpted it seems that God must have lent a hand. I almost need to shield my eyes every time." He seemed overwhelmed.

"Frankly, Mo, I wouldn't know an oak from a maple," said Zena. "To me, one acorn looks exactly like the next."

"You will learn. Such a smart girl, this will be easy. Come on and we'll walk. I will escort you around. That will show you if nothing else does."

They strolled onward, across the park, past the newly reconditioned clay tennis courts, down toward scruffy baseball diamonds. In the distance, Morris saw what once had been a second set of shuffleboard courts – with towering floodlights surrounding them, no less.

"Bubeleh, feast your eyes on that sight!" exclaimed Morris.

Zena walked cautiously across the street, sidestepping an eclectic array of motorcycles, scooters, bicyclists, and joggers. "You could kill yourself just getting to the other side of the road," she said.

"You sound more like Mendel every day. Maybe that's why I like you. But, in terms of looks, you got him hands down."

"Shush." She elbowed him in the side and waved him off.

Several park regulars greeted Morris, and a few even asked for Mendel. Zena was secretly delighted to observe the festivities which included a sexy rollerblading young woman, wearing a T-shirt saying "Save the Strand"; an older couple (but a good ten to fifteen years younger than she) strolling arm in arm; a man with a neatly trimmed salt and pepper goatee and shaved scalp. The child atop his shoulders beat rhythmically upon his head. Teen-aged wannabe basketball stars dribbled in-between cars as they ambled toward nearby hoops.

Morris repeatedly boasted, "This is one of my playing partners, Zena!" with great pride. She nodded politely to each comer and watched, surreptitiously, the nearby game. Zena warmed to the scene as the parade of friends continued.

After a short while, Morris led her toward the swimming pool area. When they were alone, she said, "Mo, they seem nice. Are any of them Jewish?"

"Some but not so many."

"Mo, there wasn't a Jewish face among them."

"Correction – one. He claimed George Jessel was an uncle by marriage on his mother's side. No, I do not know exactly what that means. But, this Jessel nephew was about to play when we left. Someday, you will meet him, I promise."

"Such a vow I do not need. Mo, I don't want involvement with an entire Gentile community."

"Zena, you are involved with me, not them, number one. Number two, Springfield happens to be a very Jewish town. I will show you around. But, before I do, number three," he paused. "I just see it all differently now. My best friends might as well be Syrians."

With care and deliberation, Morris led Zena, step by step, through the park. They traveled first around a portion of the perimeter and then cut back through the heart of the grounds.

They paused at a carefully manicured green that Zena assumed had something to do with golf. "People come up from Connecticut for matches here," said Morris. "Lawn bowling is very much the rage."

"Like bocce ball, you mean, Mo?"

"I suppose. Truth is I don't know the precise difference."

They walked on and passed by a series of ponds before hiking up a long, gentle slope. Morris ushered Zena toward the street. "My house is not far away."

"Well, it is nice but probably like a hundred other city parks," said Zena.

"No, that's where you are mistaken. Not one other park could hold a candle to this one in its youth. Olmsted, remember, did Central Park and many more aside from this one. No, this area makes me feel like I'm in the country. Urban, yes, but old suburbs. Something like Shaker Heights where I was raised. Except this park, with its trees, streams, all of that water, sets it apart. Some place this is, Zena."

"He did not create this Forest Park. And just how long have you been here, Mo?"

"Ah, a different question. And the answer to that one is too long. Before you came into my life, I was thinking that I would sell at the end of this year. I could be renting. I would be able to find something up here or one of those million places they're building for seniors like us. Would you not enjoy taking a bus ride into the city?" She did not answer.

So, they began a life together. Each day Morris and Zena trundled off to the shuffleboard courts where they played for a while. Morris had toyed forever with trick shots and wanted Zena to indulge in a game of PIG. One player had to match the other player's shot. Zena capitulated but was, not so secretly, highly competitive. She wanted the real thing. On an ambitious morning, they would stop at the nearby Dunkin' Donuts, always ordering two frosted coffee rolls for Morris and a sour cream and onion bagel, dry, for Zena.

Slowly, Zena accustomed herself to the environment and began to explore the Forest Park district for herself. Her first task was finding the right synagogue, one which felt comfortable to her. If the world were a perfect place, she would have wished each rabbi to interview with her before she selected the temple of her choice.

One afternoon, she came home and announced to Morris, "I've found it at last. It is called the Jewish Community Center and I was hooked immediately."

"So, I've been there plenty times. Swimming, cards. But, it's expensive and you can swim other places."

"Well, I met people I like immediately – in the parking lot. And programs like luncheon talks, make it/take it crafts, pool time just for seniors. At least I didn't feel like some forgotten minority when I was inside. They say they go on trips together. Shows and seaports and the like. Since we left Florida, there aren't many of us, Morris, people our age."

"I still don't see what the big deal is," he said.

"What they don't have makes it a big deal for me. Let me translate for you. I see myself, over there, turning their so-so, lukewarm program into, what, the big time, maybe? That, you see, is what I have done with my life. I move from place to place. As soon as something gets off the ground, I go elsewhere. Gypsy-like, don't you think?"

"Suppose I understand what you're saying, Zena, even if I have no idea of what that means for us. So, what are you going to do here?"

"A film series. Then, an actual movie in which these people, I hope some will become friends, can document their lives. We will have classes they can teach and take, both. Not just a listing but something more substantial in which they invest themselves. You see, this has always been my dream. When I was young, I wanted to start a school of my own but it never happened. A dream unfulfilled. Shuffleboard, yes, I love. But my passion is education. So now, people seventy, eighty, ninety and beyond need each day to matter."

"What are your qualifications? You are some authority?"

"I have experience in Florida and before that. I begin something and I will follow through with it. People like me and they want to feel the worth of going on. Gilda and I organized an entire condominium in Miami last year. We were thinking of a consulting business. That was before you two came along."

"Well, now you have a chance to expand to the Northeast, Zena. What did I tell you to start with?"

"You have some way of twisting things around, Mo. No wonder you were hard to live with."

"Is that what Mendel said? He doesn't have the inside word on my private life."

"My lips are sealed," said Zena.

The conversation concluded, Zena went back to the Jewish center to talk about a schedule and some of her course ideas. The welcome for her was warm and genuine. She was given a desk in the corner of a classroom. Zena was openly thrilled to receive her own space. She was used to making do with portable cardboard boxes serving as a traveling office.

Her enthusiasm rubbed off on Morris, who nonetheless feigned lack of interest. He, too, had become dissatisfied with his lifestyle. He had been living off savings and Social Security benefits. For years, it seemed, he would play some shuffleboard, kibitz with Mendel, eat at mealtime and in-between, watch television, and go to sleep. Simple.

Now, Zena nagged him, implored him to eat better, read more often. She said, "Neither eat nor read trash." Zena never expected him to formulate the sort of scheme he outlined to her early one fall evening as they marked their Springfield anniversary at one month, exactly.

"Zena, I am going into business. A shop of my own."

"You, a business? Dream on, Mo."

"Why not? This is about as likely as you organizing condominiums or carving a niche at the JCC."

"Mo, dear, a business involves money which, according to everything you have told me for weeks, you don't have much of. My organizing, as you put it, has been on a volunteer basis. I get nothing but satisfaction out of it."

Morris kicked at the ground as he had since he was a small child whenever he was perplexed. Seldom would he throw a tantrum but, like a frustrated dog, he pawed repeatedly.

"Would you at least hear me out? I have been working on this, inside my brain, all the while as you have been traipsing around."

"Fair enough, go ahead and spill," said Zena.

"An old people's boutique, a store but only for people our age. Not only to buy and sell but socialize, mingle, shmooz. Really, a place for everyone's investment. Our own building," he said. "New turf for the old."

"I see a senior citizens center," said Zena. "What's new about that?"

"Not quite. No hospital, antiseptic feel to it. I want warmth, and, let's face it, if I actually ran it for business purposes, that wouldn't hurt anyone. Some kind of sliding scale, though, would allow all to be included."

"So give me a few specifics, Mo."

"I'm talking games, movies, classes….the real questions, too. Where are we going? Why have we been here so long? What is our purpose? So, yes, in some ways, like any center but much more than that. Existence, Zena. But, not all mind-oriented. I want food. All my life I have dreamt bookstore/café."

"Where are you going to find people in this area to support you and this? I've been here one month and I don't see money bags right and left," she said.

"Zena, this is not Florida, thank God. No, we don't have wealthy, retired Jews at every turn. Some are here, true. Why is it so important that we attract the well-to-do? Now, of all times, we need to realize that we are not the chosen people. We do not hold a monopoly."

"So, what is it you're talking – a mixed club, a scene as the kids say. Except for anyone over seventy and does that include people who cannot dance or walk?"

"Not necessarily," he said, avoiding her question.

"Mo, once word is out all of this city's worst will be here: bag ladies, beggars, bums, everyone on the street. I saw them that first tour of downtown you gave me."

"It's all right with me that you're not interested. Just don't stand in the way. I can make this a success by myself."

"Well, I didn't quite mean I wasn't interested," said Zena. "You see, in these situations I almost always need to play devil's advocate. I did so with Gilda -- which sometimes became too much since she never could detect just where I stood on an issue." Zena took Morris's hand in both of hers. "Without prying, one final question: Where does the money come from to start the store?"

"Who says I'm buying anything? Maybe I can rent. If not, there's always Mendel."

"Oh, now I see," said Zena. "And, I imagine, if not Mendel, then my sister? Just when I was beginning to enjoy a life without her, for once. You see, we've always been in the snapshot together."

"I am not certain we need either of them," he said. "But, without something up front, we'll be paying a couple grand, I bet, for some dump that won't make anyone proud."

"Just how do you know all of this, Mr. Big?"

"Research."

"What homework could you have possibly done? And research maven, just how much would it cost to buy a building?"

"That depends, obviously, on the space you need," said Morris. "You want multiple storefronts, you're into this thing for half a million dollars or more. We're talking subdivisions. On the other hand, if you settle for a tiny, cozy out-of-spotlight location, you can maybe get it for between fifty and a hundred thousand dollars."

By now Zena was furiously pumping her head up and down. "No fooling, huh, Mo? I don't know of stores for old people, but all of these centers, even temples, stock things we want. It's tricky. You can't go in unless you're old, nu? But, if you admit you're old, you come face to face with frailties you probably never knew you had. Not to mention what all of this leads to...."

"Meaning?"

"Nursing homes, assisted living, debilitating illnesses, savings dry up, the smiling reaper awaits....Bad enough all of this is in itself without drawing even further attention to it."

Morris took Zena by both shoulders and pressed her to him. "My dear, it is something undeniable. Last time I looked, immortality is not an option – under no health plan whatsoever. You face it and live with it. Or, you are more miserable in denial. I have to believe you know this as well as I do. My father, may he rest, when I was a little boy, he used to say to me, 'Moishkie,' and he could only talk in broken English, 'when I get even older, I hope I remember nothing.' But, I knew he was far too smart for that line he fed me over and over again. It meant that he did not want to live as a cripple, in such a decrepit state."

Zena shook her head as if to brush him off. "Okay, so we better get in touch with Mendel," she said, with energy rather than resignation.

"Why this one hundred and eighty degree turn -- such a complete change of heart, Zena?"

"You know what Gilda always says about me: 'She may be wrong but, this one, she will step back, listen, and change her mind.' Maybe you got a good idea. If you want help, we need to figure out just what to put into this store."

"Here is a short list, from memory: medical supplies, hand and foot warmers, Jewish dailies from New York, fancy and warm hats, bikes with three wheels and baskets in the front, magnifying and reading glasses – plain and designer. All of that to start."

"Mo, that's fine but we need categories. Some of those items have nothing to do with others. How about a theme or even a plan?"

"Let me continue. Shuffleboard equipment, games like checkers or chess for those still with it, jigsaw and crossword puzzles. Mind games, board games like Clue and Trivial Pursuit....."

Zena interrupted. "Speaking of shuffleboard, shouldn't you coordinate with the wonderful clubhouse you and Mendel were always talking up? You want my advice, maybe you should call Mendel."

"Two minutes ago, you told me to steer clear of him on account of your sister. You know what they say, Zena, about getting off the pot or...."

"I told you to call. This is now and I have changed my mind. Go ahead or I might switch back," she added.

He stared at her. "Just remember that you gave me the okay on this. On second thought, let's go to dinner first before I try to reach Mendel."

It was later in the evening when Morris proceeded with a call to his longtime friend. The skinny man was in the tub, his head propped up on a floating air pillow, book in hand, as the telephone rang. He had brought in a cordless just in case. Mendel detested missing phone calls. It greatly vexed him that recent answering machine messages all came in muffled and fuzzy.

"What are you doing, trying to electrocute yourself, you shlemiel?" asked Morris.

"For your information, I have just engaged in a certain strenuous physical activity. Movement like this would put any man in your condition under for a serious period of time," replied Mendel.

Morris felt the blood rushing to his face and head. He stood up and gestured, all the while he was on the phone with Mendel. "So that's what it is. You think I'm a bed-ridden nothing? Zip your lips and forget that talk, Mendel. I happen to have tightened myself up, just for your own information. Anyway, I got something to talk about and since neither of us has taken the time to call or write the other, here is a start."

"Some introduction. What's on your mind? Shoot."

"I want to open a business." Morris awaited response to his opening. He held the phone away from his ear. Silence. He continued, "A specialty store for people like us, on the other side of, say, seventy-five."

"You are crazy. Nuts. No one would go."

"Maybe a sweet café, too."

"Sweets I can see you with. Otherwise, I don't know where you got this idea – from Zena – or what?"

"Leave her out of this. I want a place for old people – a joint not so much like a hospital or independent living. A place not simply to play cards like some center or something but a spot where people also listen to music of their choice. They have such places, I hear, for teenagers. Not for geezers like us. We could stock items. Fur lined gloves with extra insulation that deals with winter. I imagine getting a whole selection of mini-fans. This would be a draw."

"Let's say your idea holds my interest for half a second. How do you finance?"

"Even if I rent, I need to borrow some money. From a person of means."

"Which is why you called me, Morris. I become a source. And, what do I get out of it?" Mendel sang.

"Your name on the marquee. Or, at least our initials. I haven't figured that out."

"I have one word for you, Morris. No."

"How about just a short term loan, Mendel, which I can repay in no time at all?"

"I'll never again see that as cash, Morris. We are out here on the island which is expensive enough."

"Mendel, we need five grand up front, for the store front, to get moving on this. That is even without extensive supplies."

"I imagine the we includes Zena. So, I am doling out to both of you. Prove to me that you two can raise something on your own. Then, maybe I listen and pitch in," he said.

"How much do I need to show?"

"A thousand bucks within a week," said Mendel.

"Mendel, we are not wealthy people with the king's resources you're dealing with. If we were, I would not be calling. Be reasonable."

"I don't deal with anybody. This is not, in case you forgot, my idea."

"Be calm, Mendel. If we can come up with some money within a few weeks, you might help out, no? Is that true?"

"Ten days. You should thank someone's God that you know me. Without me, as I have been saying for years, you are nowhere. Let me be. I am getting ready for Gilda."

"Suit yourself and keep it to yourself, Mendel." And with that, Morris slammed down the telephone.

Zena timidly touched his elbow but he recoiled as if in shock. "What was that all about?" she asked. "He, of course, will not help, but that cannot have stunned you. You look like a bolt of lightning shot through you. He cares only about himself, right?"

"Not so much that," said Morris. "Mendel needs us to show him our worth, our mettle by raising quick money. Then, he'll match and more than that. He is no fool and will eventually lend out plenty."

"That sounds reasonable – we talking a few hundred?"

"Try one thousand. More even."

"That's a bit different. Where do we get it, Mo?"

"Zena, I can get my hands on that much. It's his attitude, as it always has been. He is a superior know it all. I could get the money, even in cash. Not the point."

She seemed oblivious, explaining that her assets were tied up in Florida, that her supply was not liquid.

"If we need the money, I can get it, Zena," he repeated.

As if on a swivel, Zena's head began bobbing up and down in assent. Morris stared at her, almost through her, thinking Zena to be a woman in her late fifties, maybe early sixties at the very most. He knew better but was not certain of her age. She had always been evasive with him on the issue. He could not recall when he had last questioned her. This much he knew: she was younger and she would live longer. When people asked him, he always told them he was around eighty. Morris knew he could get by for a while longer. He thought about what it would mean to marry Zena and then die, leaving her alone. Not so; she had Gilda. Well, she said she was tired of Gilda and their dependence upon one another.

It was an expression of endearment Zena wore upon her sweet face, a pure and trusting look that Morris could not possibly resist. Leaning in to her, he realized Zena was a woman he could love and who could love him. No, this was precious and not easy to come by. The corners of his lips turned gently upward and Morris knew that she had become a part of him, as he was of her.

"Zena, you listen, so that I can elaborate upon my plan."

"Morris Greenbaum, you are a man of guts and passion. Dream on. Certainly, I would be glad to listen," she said, gazing at him as if he were some youthful Romeo.

"What we need is a major deal, a blowout benefit for the store. Before we lose our shirts and whatever else, we need to advertise, have a shindig no one will ever forget. The event itself will be some kind of promotion and it will propel us, lift us off the runway."

"Go on."

"What about a challenge match – anyone can play who is maybe sixty-five or more? Or, set up a colossal clash between the men of the Forest Park Shuffleboard Club and the women representing the Jewish Community Center. You're forming a team so let's see what you have. That sort of package."

"Assuming I bury my competitive drive and let's just say I go for this scheme, how exactly do we make money?"

"Charge everybody. We have registration fees for players, tickets for those who watch. And, we organize a concession stand. We get Park and Rec to give clearance. Of course, we do not turn away anyone who cannot pay."

"Mo, we're not working with millionaires here. You're talking about some people who no longer earn a daily wage and they haven't nest eggs either. I bet a few only get out once a week. What's wrong with you?"

"Well, we have to charge something. So, even if it's a few shekels, that's something to take in. Of course, if we get some of those affluent types as a balance, for example, we're in the money. You know that, Zena?"

"You're some character. But, how are those suburban people going to get here? No one has money – not towns, nor residents. Leftovers from Kennedys and Rockefellers, the oil people in the Middle East. They got money. As one of them was gloating on some TV news program lately, they control us, not the other way around."

"You know so much, Zena, just like Mendel, what do you suggest?" asked Morris as beads of sweat formed above his bushy brows. He reddened, growing brighter by the moment until he could feel the rush of blood in his face.

"I am not trying to say don't do it, Mo. A part of me always calls the question." With that, she hugged him tightly, and Morris felt himself melting within her grasp.

***

Assembling a representative team proved more daunting than Zena had anticipated. Previously, her touch had been golden. Women who knew Zena wanted to play with her, for her. Others wished to learn. All knew that Zena could teach almost anyone to play shuffleboard.

Now, however, with the festival planned for the end of September, Zena had just more than a month to gather players, prime them, select complementary partners, and ultimately field a squad.

Zena easily designated a number one doubles team. Gert Sirota could play any man even up and Midge Schwartz, an all-around athlete who competed in Senior Games, would complete that team.

Then, the drop-off began. Lil Pincus had some potential but could not see past her face. Recently, she had discarded Coke bottle eyeglasses she found too embarrassing to wear and chose Lasik surgery. Virtually guaranteed to work for all patients, the procedure left Lil with perpetual red-eye and blurred vision. Zena thought she might play with Lil and, with any luck, bag many a win at second doubles. Besides, Zena liked Lil for dressing up, showing off, taking pride in her wardrobe. Unlike others, she didn't wear stiff, outdated slacks and blouses. Lil was fit but she could not discern the numbers on the opposite triangle before letting a disk fly. Still, Zena and Lil would cope.

The third team was not so fortunate. Zena knew, having watched her from behind, that Sarah Moskowitz was far too wide and bulky to handle a cue. Her sister, Shelly Levin, complained of chronic back pain. "It travels up and down, all around," she would explain, seizing any opportunity to speak without prompting.

Rita Gross and Dot Kramer, vying for the final spot on the team, had more serious problems. Rita balanced herself with a cane while playing. Dorothy, healthy of mind and body, was absolutely uncoordinated. She could not cajole even a solitary disk onto the court.

Accustomed to efficiency and accountability, Zena took her position seriously and announced practices to be held three times per week. She put Sarah Moskowitz on the Lewis version of the Scarsdale Diet, allowing one cookie every so often as incentive and reward. Sarah began to lose immediately although she remained quite overweight. Zena ordered arthritic Shelley to ditch herbal remedies and, instead, apply Ben gay, a heating pad, and stretch more often.

Sooner rather than later, the squad assumed its identity. Zena imagined moderate success and she talked about prospects often and at length. Morris found her attention to task a bit too functional and reprimanded her. Besides, he had more pressing concerns.

Two months in advance, Morris finally announced the tourney challenge to the men. Having gone to the park each day for a couple of months, he made mental notes regarding possible pairings. Morris hesitated, however, because he had not yet formulated a lucrative, alluring package. Besides, the players were not, for the most part, Jewish, and while Morris could care less, he worried about implications. In fact, only Cy Avram, Orthodox no less, played at the park. And Cy's schedule was somewhat determined by holy days. Moreover, Morris and Cy, having once viciously debated the merits of belly vs. Nova lox, had never really gotten along. Cy was adamant in his preference for belly and did not believe Morris's claim to have been raised on Nova in Shaker Heights.

One morning Morris, having pondered forever, dropped his invitation upon his peers. "Boys, my lady friend who coaches a new shuffleboard team at the Jewish Community Center, asked if I could round up a group for a challenge against some of her women. I told her that, just for fun, we would take up arms, so to speak. Don't disappoint me here. What say?" Morris cupped his ear. "We need two topnotch teams."

Teddy Shawn, as ever, seized the opportunity. "Sure, Maurice, and I bet you got some extra activity in mind? Out with it. You know girls better than us, that we always assume."

Morris, the ringleader of the band, was quite prepared for Teddy's dig. Morris easily brushed aside harmless digs. Shawn, realizing the Maurice bit perturbed Morris, went right after the big man with the gentle taunt. Morris did not react but, instead, stared ahead while preparing his reply.

"I thought we might make you, Teddy, captain of the squad, which means going up against the ladies' best."

"I ain't never paired off with no Jewish girl," said Shawn, flexing his still muscular forearm to show off his Navy tattoo, a sexy mermaid. An admiral during World War II and current leader of the local VFW chapter, he simply could not resist another title. "Provided I can whip these old farts into competitive shape, and we will. Right, Kiley?" Teddy motioned toward a lean, well-dressed man. His white hair was carefully groomed as was an accompanying mustache which seemed etched and attached to his upper lip. Kiley was forever Shawn's trustworthy consultant. He rarely questioned the leader even if he, Kiley, was by far the more perceptive of the two men.

During the next month, Shawn and Kiley worked so smoothly that Morris was able to retreat and tend to logistical details of the match. Perhaps because of his bulk and bluster, local officials, suddenly congenial, went along with Morris's suggestions: move bleachers in so that onlookers could get a bird's eye view of the proceedings; slap together a makeshift ticket booth; bring in a volunteer, amateur band; split profits with the city on concession products (such as T-shirts and bumper stickers) to be sold at the event.

As the big day approached, with Kiley at his side, Shawn walked with renewed swagger and spoke with great bravado. Morris caught himself wondering whether the women, whom he previously thought would trounce the men, stood a chance.

Zena, more often audacious, grew uncharacteristically passive. "We are coming along, but very slowly, at a snail's pace," she said, one week before the event. "Shelley threw out her back the other day and can't walk, let alone practice. Sarah slipped off her diet and put on five pounds in, seemingly, five minutes. You may think that's a good joke but I want a team that will put those men in their proper place." Morris grimaced and smacked his hands together.

The next day Morris planted himself on the rickety wooden bench by the outside courts. He carried a laptop computer but realized someone would have to create a program for him. Knowing little about computers, Morris was the first to realize he was in trouble going solo.

"Kiley, name your team players," said Morris.

"Kiley and Gamelli, match one; Shawn and Knight, match two; Avram and Bigsby, match three."

"You sure Avram can play? It's the Sabbath."

"He told me the rabbi would consider. Avram feels he will receive permission since we go so late in the afternoon. I would have thought you would know this, Morris," said Kiley, simultaneously straightening his vest with his left hand while slicking down his mustache with his right thumb and index finger.

"I am what you call a country boy Jew. I don't know from laws of kosher nor keeping Saturday holy. My family went to synagogue for

High Holy Days and we celebrated Chanukah, Passover, and maybe Purim. To tell the truth, Henry, you probably know more about my religion than I do. Yet, I am sincere and I do not hide my ignorance. That counts for something?"

"Morris, you certainly know more about Judaism than I. Thank you, by the way, for using my first name. Avram, in any case, expects to play." Kiley spoke with an authoritative air as if he were a seasoned stage actor.

***

Morris thrashed about in bed the night before the challenge match. He had placed articles in daily, weekly, and alternative papers, not to mention inter-state reminder newsletters. He convinced the PBS, ABC, and NBC local affiliates to list the contest in calendars. He advertised in churches, temples, nursing homes, assisted and independent living residences, senior centers, and even through bridge clubs. He traveled to malls within thirty or forty minutes, which included many across the Connecticut state line. All the while, Morris hadn't any idea of whether he would draw five, fifty or a hundred people.

He planned to charge three dollars admission and another buck for a raffle – not to mention the concession stand. It was easy, with Zena's help, to convince the Jewish Community Center to kick in supplies.

Morris, during rare idle moments, could not help but wonder whether Mendel was avoiding him. The men hadn't spoken for weeks, and Morris felt the strain as he feared his closest friendship was in jeopardy.

Zena, in the meantime, had become overly exhausted through her teaching, motivating, organizing. Instead of making the most of her last moments before the match, she fell asleep early that evening and did not awaken until she heard Morris thumping about in the bedroom before dawn the following morning.

"Mo," she whispered in a scratchy voice, "Mo, there's nothing more you can do. The match will catch everyone's fancy – something nobody around here has ever seen, don't you worry about that. Take my advice, Mo, and go back to sleep."

"Zena, the sun's not coming up. If it rains, we are flummoxed. I have no serious alternative. I've been counting on good weather all the while."

"What are you talking? We have next Saturday as the rain date," she said, turning over.

"I know, I know. But Zena, if this thing falls like a lead balloon, what then?"

"Then, we are back where we started – which, if you need a translation, means each of us is in much better shape than before we met." He shrugged his large shoulders and glanced at her. "I meant minds, not silhouettes," she explained. She tapped him on the head as if he were a cuddly Saint Bernard in order to calm his nerves.

"If only we had met thirty years ago, Zena."

"Your Ruthie, according to what you've told me, would not have approved, not exactly," sang Zena, in nasal tones.

Morris was not eager to invoke Ruth's name. "If you don't mind let's leave her out of it," he said as he swept his hand upward.

Morris and Zena, working as a team, took the full morning for set up. A flashy eye-catching banner would do wonders for the store. Zena convinced the senior art class at the JCC to paint a mural, with glowing shuffleboard courts in the background. Morris, unconvinced that anyone could meet his standards, took care of preparation and preliminary cleanup himself, including raking, sweeping, and disposal.

Zena departed at eleven to find, organize, and finally spur her players to task. Morris was left to check on details. The city had offered him the service of a park policeman but Morris balked. Now, he changed his mind and was forced, by himself, to locate and cajole the cop.

The weather bureau and a local television station, both of which he telephoned, claimed unsettled conditions would prevail in the area, but no one could predict when afternoon showers might begin. Leave it up to them, thought Morris. They could never make a firm call. If they were wrong, they would, no doubt, claim a sudden pattern shift had taken them unaware.

By twelve-thirty, Zena arrived back on the scene with her van of players. They wore classy white knit shirts and royal blue trousers with white stripes running along the sides. Each player's name was monogrammed above the shirt pocket. She had kept all of this, including the cost, hidden from Morris.

Shawn and Kiley's crew looked somewhat ragged – as if they sensed the worst. The lieutenant, himself, had dressed to the hilt: he selected a matching velour outfit including crimson top and silver bottom. The rest of the men, though, were not nearly so striking. Two of them chose shorts, a decision which prognosticated muggy, tropical conditions. Gamelli's were baggy while Knight's fit too snugly around the waist. Shawn had either forgotten or avoided shaving. Ever-disheveled Avram looked as if he had just rolled out of bed and onto the floor. His curly dark hair stuck in a large mass on one side but appeared perfectly coiffed on the other. He might have been a scarecrow, a Yiddish one yet.

Zena walked defiantly around the court perimeter to shake an embarrassed Kiley's hand. Acting nonplussed, he bowed, feigning ease. Zena, steadying the man's quaking hand, knew better.

"We'll just see what happens during the match. That's what really counts," she said, as if to console. Kiley twice bobbed his head up and down while Shawn hobnobbed about in vain, hoping to bring an ordered look to the men's team.

Soon it would be a quarter of one and Morris was in a panic. Not even a dozen spectators had arrived. Morris imagined Mendel's mockery of the scene, visualizing his best friend's callow, crooked quiver of his turkey neck and cylindrical head – the bony shoulders. Morris could not have been more disgusted – at the turnout, his own lack of cool and preoccupation with Mendel.

Morris lumbered off to the rear park entrance, muttering to himself of lost opportunity, the demise of the Forest Park elephant, polar bear, lions (a rumor), and wild birds. He lamented the state of the park, missed the radiance of peacocks he once saw strut their elegant stuff. Now, instead, broken bottles made it an impossibly tough go for bikers, rollerbladers, runners, and walkers. Through the reverie, he floated pleasantly backward in time.

Suddenly, a long, blue vehicle approached the Trafton Road entrance to the grand park. It was filled with animated men and women. Morris began trotting toward the playing site. As he reached the courts, a squat SUV, occupied by another contingent of seniors, stopped at the main gate checkpoint. Spectators tumbled out of the vehicle and Morris, recalling a favorite gesture he utilized to emphasize his height rather than girth, sucked in his breath. He greeted all, chatted up future clientele, helped everyone find a seat, and only then realized he hadn't collected money for tickets. In his haste, he had not arranged for ticket booth coverage. Taking money while shmoozing would not work.

Instead, he reached into his pocket, produced a wad of printed coupon tickets and went around asking for donations. Morris held an orange and purple can in one hand and pressed towards himself a stack of programs listing team participants. He wedged the papers between his elbow and chest. He had written in an entrance fee of three dollars on the can and at the top of the program but when people asked what to give, he always relied, "We need funding. But, only if you got something you can spare."

The new carousel had become the park's jewel. Donated by a local philanthropist, it spun round and round in the midst of playing fields. Morris could only hear (vaguely at that) the deep, rhythmic beat of the organ in the background. Groups of kids scurried across a distant baseball diamond. With each stride, they came closer to the merry-go-round. Morris, for just one moment, felt transported backward to Cleveland, the city of his boyhood, where he was raised between the two world wars.

Reality interrupted the daydream. Morris, quickly computing, surmised that the kids must have adults tagging along behind them. All of them could easily become spectators for his event. Delighted with the prospect, he audibly thanked God for the weather, blessed his own luck, and clenched his fist in the manner of his idol, Jackie Gleason.

Just then, Zena grabbed at his fleshy waist, and whispered into his ear, "Mo, come on and step to it. It's past one and we need to begin, huge throng or no. And, I'll tell you something, my girls will outclass these shlumps like nothing a Midwesterner ever saw."

He raised his bushy eyebrows, which came together when he looked upward, "Bet you an ice cream cone."

"A piece of strudel."

"Whatever you say."

Zena returned to her team members, who were busy doing stretches and, according to individual capabilities, more exotic warm-up exercises. Urged to become creative and uninhibited, the players took seriously the coach's advisories.

On the other hand, the men stood about muttering to one other. They talked about the odds of winning, the ladies' physical attributes. They might as well have been college freshmen. The Forest Park boys tried their hardest to appear at ease, even nonchalant. It was clear, however, that virtually all were anxious.

"Ladies and gentlemen," Morris boomed, without aid of microphone or megaphone. "You are about to witness a match between a fine women's contingent, "Zena Lewis' JCC Shufflers" versus "Special K: That's Shawn and Kiley's FP Shuffleboard Club.

"Why, you may ask, is such a match transpiring? Here is the answer. With the proceeds, I, Morris Kahn, plan to open a specialty store and café for, if you do not mind, slightly older people, mostly slightly older people, that is. In order to move off our own dime, forgive me, we need some dough. We have to get a capital base. Your contributions, together with outside resources, will boost our spirits and hopes. If you like what you see, drop off whatever you can at the ticket booth later on. Meanwhile, enjoy!"

Team members lined up to shake hands. The seemingly terse, tense women relaxed while the men, jocular during preliminaries, grew rigid with fear, jittery with nervous energy. Roles, not surprisingly, had suddenly reversed.

Kiley stepped up to shoot first. He addressed the cue meticulously, then drew it to his lips as if he might covertly whisper instructions. He tugged on the red grip and confidently pushed the first crimson disk but it landed well short of marked areas in the triangle across the way. Kiley shook his hand slightly, smiled ruefully, and sat.

Gert Sirota, up next, patiently planted a disk directly in a seven slot. Rich Gamelli, stubby, dark, immensely loyal to those he considered family, had lived in the South End of the city most of his life before recently moving up the hill to an apartment house near the park. Gamelli knew how to conduct himself around women and saluted Gert before taking his own shot. She giggled in return. Gamelli, a sportsman who often went to the rifle range on Sunday mornings, twice saluted Gert with his open hand.

Dashing, he whistled the disk past the court and onto the grass beyond. Midge Schwartz, meanwhile, wearing blue Nike walking shoes which complemented her outfit, pasted a snappy shot in the eight triangle, thereby protecting her teammate's seven for safekeeping.

The first match progressed smoothly as Midge and Gert diligently piled up points while Kiley and Gamelli suffered. Before each shot, the Italian either bowed respectfully or doffed his cap with a sweeping gesture. He eyed the two women, correctly sensing that, to them, he could be a catch of the day. Kiley, the clinician, suggested techniques to Gamelli.

"Bend your back," he coaxed. "Finesse, man, no hurry, no blasting in this zone." Kiley himself had not scored a single point and could barely watch as Midge and Gert zoomed to twenty-five. Only Gamelli's lucky ten kept the men within distance of a win.

Teddy Shawn yelled with a combination of encouragement and threat: "Don't disgrace us, Kiley! It's your kind of day – nice and hot," he added, smirking.

The women, too, kept up the banter. Rita Gross and Dot Kramer, alternates, led courteous, more moderate cheers: "Show 'em how to do it, sis!" they yelled. "Old girls, gray girls, better this way, girls," they said, eyeing one another. No one knew quite what they meant.

Before long, the contest was over and Kiley trudged off, smoothing his trousers, grinding his teeth in dismay. He held his head high but the veins in his neck betrayed his disappointment. Still, the crowd erupted with a lengthy cheer. To those who watched, it was the game that mattered rather than winners or losers. The little Italian, Gamelli, ate up the applause, bowing low, nearly scraping his protruding potbelly on the ground in recognition. Zena, for her part, was quietly satisfied, secretly smug.

Captain Ted Shawn and Henry Knight, next up, were poised to compete against player-coach Zena Lewis and Lil Pincus, a woman not five feet in height. Without her spectacles, she could not see more than a few paces in front of her. Of course, Lil claimed she could carry on without the glasses. Ever prepared, Zena brought along a strap. The fastening device allowed Lil to dangle her eyeglasses about her neck in between shots. She had that luxury.

Lil began play without wearing the glasses. After missing the disk entirely, then poking it clear out of bounds on a subsequent attempt, her shoulders drooped. Concluding that inferior play, though, was a greater embarrassment than binocular-like glasses, Lil fetched hers and perched them halfway down her nose.

Zena, the ultimate competitor, came out flying on the runway, landing two tens in succession. Teddy Shawn matched. Cigarette dangling from his lips all the while, cancer be damned as he often said, Shawn maintained the steadiest of hands. He had taken up the sport with a scientist's zeal. A former engineer who had never been particularly athletic, Shawn had gone so far as to chart grades of sloping cement. This he accomplished by himself when no one else but a few cops wandered about in the park. Shawn loved solitary moments when he could concentrate so specifically and intensely. He kept computerized data to record his discoveries.

On this day, Teddy stuck all the disks in spaces during his opening round, leading his team to a hard-fought six point victory: fifty-two to forty-six.

Lil, lenses in hand, bolted up to shake the victors' hands. She and Zena had played well, but lost. Zena seemed unaffected, that is until she spied Morris leaning upon the ticket booth, bent over at the waist from laughter. He winked at her but she cried, "Be quiet Mo and just wait!"

Cy Avram, limbering up by performing jumping jacks as he had been instructed in the sixth grade, was eventually ready to play. His current Rabbi Lipsky had suggested that the entire event was total foolishness, but Cy was determined to compete. He and Sailor Bigsby, so-called for his two Navy hitches (amounting to eight years), were opposed by Sarah Moskowitz, who munched chocolate chips between shots, and her little sister, Shelley Levin, the hypochondriac.

Shelley led off with a good seven but Avram bumped her off the court, replacing her disk with his. Sarah Moskowitz missed everything on her first shot, then landed a good eight of her own. Sailor Bigsby fired hard but bounced one off the back wooden frame of the court and into the ten off zone. "Sombitch!" he yelled. "Hit the end board – don't count."

"By my rules, it's ten off. You're in the kitchen, boychik," said Shelley, suddenly free of nagging pain.

Sailor was immediately defensive. "Hey, Kiley, where did you find her, this one who claims she got special rules?"

Avram waived his hand, a calming gesture. "I know her family and she is one girl from hearty stock. A good Jewish lady is what she is."

"Religion never interested me," said Bigsby. "No, winning is the object here, winning this match. And, she is out to stop us," he added, adjusting the sailor cap he always wore.

Shelley's second shot landed just short of the ten triangle. Avram, shooting for eight, misfired and tipped Shelley's disk ever so slightly, nudging it into the ten spot.

"Atta boy!" belted Sarah Moskowitz before stepping up. "That's what we need." She then hooked one off to the side.

Sailor Bigsby urged a disk into the eight slot but cussed himself loudly for not having shoved Shelley out of the way.

Thus, the match seesawed back and forth until the final round. Shelley led off and nailed a beauty – right smack in the center of the seven space. "Bingo!" she chortled. Avram matched her with a nifty shot that landed in the opposite rectangle. Sarah Moskowitz, breathing deeply and gulping water before her turn, steadied sufficiently to place an eight. Bigsby, his competitive fire stoked, hit for a ten. The scoreboard, manned by two passersby, showed a tie: fifty-three all.

What now? Morris hadn't planned for this eventuality – a tie. He announced quickly, as if from recitation, that "we will now play one quick game with a rule change – first to twenty-five wins!"

"That's baloney, I never heard of such a rule, Kahn," yelled Bigsby, one of the very few who knew Morris by his last name.

"You winded?" taunted Sarah Moskowitz before Zena could shush her. "Bagby, you're not in such tip-top shape as you thought."

"Ah ha, the oversized vacuum cleaner speaks," jeered Bigsby. And that was just the start of the repartee.

Everyone was pressured, no one could score. Not that the players had lost touch. Rather, they began to shoot at one another's disks. Even those first up sought to block by positioning the disks at the head of the ten triangle. The defensive struggle, complete with built-in obstacles, was on. After a few rounds of this business, Morris grew testy.

"Must we lower the score for sudden death to, say, eight? Come on, somebody score, dammit!" he roared, immediately sorry that he sounded quite so enraged. In truth, he was somewhat amused.

Bigsby quickly scored with two red disks, each a seven, but neither girl could find the mark. Avram blocked one of his teammate's shots, ensuring some points. Suddenly, the men were up by fourteen.

Zena called for time to counsel her women. "Don't worry about them. They're old, they're overconfident, and, besides, they can't perform, probably in any way," she pronounced, drawing loud laughter. "Shoot your match and we'll be fine." Following her advice, the girls quickly drew to within a point. Nervous but determined, they barely managed to outscore the men and thus created a tie.

"So much for that. It is over," called Morris. "We are now dead even. Enough!" He issued the blunt statement with authority and without exasperation. Sarah Moskowitz, for one, was delighted. She knew she could not have continued for much longer.

Morris asked the crowd if it wanted more, and the swell of applause ringing in his ears, he urged, then physically pushed the players back onto the courts. This time, though, Zena and Lil lined up opposite Shawn and Knight.

Crucial moments of high drama might very well mark the match. Bigsby and Sarah Moskowitz were far more interested in insulting one another than playing. Kiley was concerned that his velour might wrinkle or soil. Avram repeatedly glanced over his shoulder, expecting a rabbinical spy to track him. Zena was smug, having affirmed a contention that her players, with just one month of practice, could stay with the men.

Morris was delighted to be making money, so pleased that he was ready to eat. In the middle of the first game of the second round, he called for a time out. No one knew why.

"You know, my friends, nobody wins here. We are all victors because everyone came, contributed and, with God's help, I will be able to open a store and café for all of us, the young oldsters. Given what happened a few years ago, what with terror in New York, bloodshed in Israel, not to mention Iraq, we should be even more thankful. Let us move on, then, to a party. I know, this comes as a surprise to all, even to my friend Zena. Shift your eyes to that field and you'll find a free carousel. Just for us. We can play as long as we like!

"Okay, call me crazy but, listen, we haven't been on a merry-go-round what, for half a century. Okay, maybe I am off by ten years. Still, we can get popcorn and soda and eat and drink all we want. Have a ball!"

Not one person moved until Lil Pincus straightened her shoulders, placed her glasses on the bridge of her nose and said, peering upward, "Well, my word, it is a carousel, just like in the movies. I am going to get that gold ring, just as I did when I was a little girl."

On the backs of wooden horses and ponies, most often clutching the reins furiously, around and around they all sped. Children again, they coasted up and down while dreams swirled about them all.

"Sarah," sang Sailor Bigsby, temporarily ditching his arrogance, "Sarah, keep your feet in the stirrups and stick, like airplane glue, to the pole."

"All right. I know what I'm doing," she snapped. And then, informally, "Okay, Joe."

"How did you come by my handle, my name?"

"Little birdies speak," she teased.

Even Avram was up and riding high, pressing his yarmulkah to his head with one hand while hugging the fake, painted horse's mane with the other. Morris rode in a simulated stagecoach with Zena, the two of them making like joyous CEO's as they surveyed the entire operation.

Morris latched onto Zena's shoulder and sighed deeply. He released years of pent up anxiety with one, prolonged breath.

"What is it Mo?"

"This is working, it is all coming together like the gears of a giant clock," he said. "Look at them all, these gray-haired, balding geezers on their golden stallions."

"Did you ever doubt that this would be such a smash?" asked Zena.

"Zena, these days I need someone like you. After the buildings tumbled, and with all I know some distant relative of mine blown up every week across the world, I am so small. And, who really knows how many years, how many days I got left? I used to think this would go on forever."

"Mo, I pretend that everything is all to the good. Little does the average Joe imagine what I'm thinking inside. You are such a little boy, at heart, even now." She kissed him lightly and fully upon the lips.

They began to embrace as a shrieking bird sent the twosome into a spin. Zena lurched but failed to locate the origin of the call. She walked against the flow, as the carousel turned, hoping to trace down the origins of the sound. Zena disappeared from Morris's view, but soon returned, trotting, with news. "It's Lil Pincus. She took off her glasses and they stuck beneath her horse. Don't worry, she's okay, but her frames are kaput. The lenses somehow survived."

Sure enough, a quaking Lil, looking even tinier, like a miniature, appeared. Still, she remained true to form. "No parrot can take me down!" she announced, for those who cared to listen.

Who knew what was next? It was hours later that Morris, two large buckets dangling by plastic handles over his wrists, prodded each participant to donate. He implored people: "Bigger please, and better."

Some people looked away, others claimed they had run out of both change and bills, but many individuals came up with something: quarters, a silver watch, a check for a hundred dollars, whatever.

Later that afternoon as he, Zena and Teddy Shawn (a most unlikely volunteer) policed the area, Morris felt certain that he had succeeded. He would show that no-good Mendel, once and for all.

Morris squeezed several hundred dollars right there in his hand. Mendel could not possibly refuse him.

CHAPTER 6

"You, you're not satisfied, what does that mean?" roared Morris, smacking his cordless phone on the kitchen table before catching it on a hop as it plummeted toward the slate floor beneath.

Mendel, on the other end of the line, held his phone six inches away from his ear. "I simply said that a clean grand was my figure and I believe you're a couple hundred bucks short," he repeated.

"Listen, you tight-fisted goy, you, this is surely the lowest of your many disgraceful moments," said Morris. "We break our behinds for more than a month and this is what we get?"

"Morris, I am more than willing to come up there and talk."

"Talk is as cheap as you are. Why do you even suggest the idea?"

"Let me see what it is you have in mind. I will come up and help you with the place. Maybe you need someone like me who's been involved in real estate for half a century. I can't part with my money on no notice," he said.

While grabbing for the receiver, Morris yelled for Zena. "He says he's coming up here. What do you think of that?"

"This is what you wanted, no?" she said.

"He snookers me, first, then you, too?"

"You know him better, Morris. You told me this is what he's like."

"Mendel, I'll call you back."

Morris smashed the phone into its case.

***

Two weeks later to the day, Mendel arrived at the airport, slick and shiny in the maroon blazer and gray slacks Gilda had purchased for him. He wore a navy blue beret and matching ascot to complement the outfit.

"Va-va-voom!" exclaimed Morris and nearly crushed his friend with a tremendous bear hug. "For someone who couldn't pass for Norton, you don't look bad," he said. "What's with these new duds? You don't look so pale, maybe even not so scrawny," he said.

"Morris, I wish I could say the same for you. You look just as fat as ever," Mendel replied.

"Same old Mendel. I tried to give you the benefit, but why? Forget about it."

"So how's my sister?" asked Zena, reaching out for Mendel's hand.

"Never been better, at least that's what she says. She did not want to accompany me under any circumstances. I couldn't tell you why. I just go solo."

"God knows why so it must be just as well," said Zena.

Mendel rejoiced that he had returned to New England, if only for the weekend. "Look at such buildings. What do you call them, porticos? We have nothing like that on Long Island. There, you got a landscape of gas stations and motels. Bowling alleys wherever you turn."

"Bowling alleys are nothing new. We had them even when I lived in Ohio," said Morris.

"Maybe so but not seventy lanes. Here, Morris, you are in God's country. It's not spoiled, like Long Island and the people there, too."

"Why do you insist on living there, Mendel?" asked Zena.

"The water, the ocean. My mind is growing dim but I seem to recall Freud saying we want to get back to the womb," said Mendel.

Morris chose scenic back roads as he drove to Springfield. This route guaranteed glimpses of Suffield, Conn., the exclusive, wealthy WASP town Morris knew Mendel could not resist. Morris wanted

Mendel by his side and would spare nothing to influence his old friend. Morris knew that Mendel adored the pristine, aristocratic quiet of a small, storybook New England town. Mendel, a city Jew, felt magnetically drawn to the bucolic. That much, Morris knew for sure. Determined to place his old confidant back at his side, Morris was conniving. He had not even told Zena that he found Mendel irreplaceable. Morris wanted both of his best friends all for himself.

Mendel had maintained ownership of the Boston duplex – the two-family house he had lived in on the opposite side of the park – giving him access to the shuffleboard courts. Mendel formerly lived in the lower apartment while keeping the upstairs vacant. Aware that he lost money with his refusal to rent, Mendel claimed he could "no longer put up with someone else's mishegoss. Bad enough that I'm half crazy most of the time. Being a landlord would send me sailing over the edge. Each man to himself. Me, I will stay to myself." That's what he used to say. Now though, before settling for a few day's at his friend's place, Mendel decided to explore the confines of his own apartment. He brought an extra valise filled with clothing and souvenirs, all of which belonged in Springfield – cherished items of the past.

"Will you look at this? Just as I left it before we went south, Morris," he said, pointing toward a rickety bookcase holding a couple of hundred volumes. "That's Sholem Aleichem and next to him is Shakespeare. Two greats, both long dead, they live side by side on my old stand."

Morris and Mendel never spent a great deal of time in one another's apartments. Morris, though, was awed by Mendel's collection of books including many Hebrew and Yiddish editions, as well as English.

"Where did you accumulate such a trove? It is mind-boggling, Mendel! I never saw you read all the time."

"Morris, a lot of things we never knew about each other. I am discovering more now, away from you. Just for your mental record on me, I never told you that, as a young man, before I went into business, I taught in a Brooklyn shul. First Hebrew, then English. For a few years after that I tried leading a great books class in public school. This is, what, fifty years ago, maybe more. How did I do it? I bought myself a lot of books then. You see them right before your eyes. Never threw out even one book, Morris."

"Then what, you made money? And you've not spent a red cent to fix up this place? It could be a palace, that much I know."

"You know so much about money, Morris? Spend your own."

"Maybe you're right. If I had some, I would. Listen, Zena is slaving over a new range back home preparing a pot roast like you never saw. Come on, let's walk across the park and indulge in this feast."

"Morris, I have a confession. Coming to Springfield, I have to stay in my own house. Otherwise, I don't feel right."

"After you eat something, we'll talk. House, shmouse, it won't matter once you get something in your stomach."

Mendel, since he did not designate food the soul and substance of his existence, knew otherwise. He appreciated Zena's kindness and told her so, but picked at his food while Morris gobbled up everything in sight. After dinner, the boys settled in front of the new, large-screen television. Clicker in hand, Morris felt supreme. Zena cleaned up. Mendel, pretending to snooze, tried to gauge the relationship before him.

Before long, everyone was dozing. Soon, they went to bed.

Next morning, Morris called his realtor at nine in the morning. Morris shook Mendel out of a deep sleep. "I got three places lined up for you, for us to see. Get your gear moving. I feel bad making the lady work on Shabbes."

"What, she's not Jewish?"

"Mendel, I don't even know. But, I feel bad. I don't like making anyone work on a Saturday. Besides, I have spent much of the past year reading, every day, The New York Times. This is no good, this year. On 9/11 the trade centers blow up, then for three years blood and death in Israel and Palestine. I never imagined such a thing as what they call a suicide bomber. You know, this John Kerry has some Jewish blood in him. Can't be all that bad."

"Shlemiel! You're the one getting hosed. This woman you hired will make out like a bandit. She cops your dollars and you worry about her. No wonder you, yourself, can't make a buck."

Zena arrived with a platter of belly lox and assorted bagels.

"Furthermore, just for your information," added Mendel, "you both complain about money and then you dish out a small fortune for lox. It goes at, what, fifteen dollars or maybe even twenty per pound. I don't like it one bit unless you got nova."

"Oh my God!" cried Zena. "I went special, all the way downtown, to get belly."

***

Caren Sussman had married into her husband's real estate company. Now, on the long side of fifty and newly widowed, she had inherited the business and its assets. Once the belle, by her account, of the high school ball, she was quite pleased that men's heads no longer snapped as she walked by. Enough of that. On the other hand, she hoped middle age would, for her, carry on for at least another fifteen years. Caren dreaded aging and what she assumed was a hole, a terrifying abyss beyond. She had lost three people, her husband's associates, when the Trade Centers fell, and she had not recovered fully. Every day, to distract herself, she thought of lifts and tucks. She went to Boston to seek out opinions. She desperately wished to obliterate the bags beneath her eyes and the cellulite on her thighs. Dreading the knife, she had not yet made the plunge.

To avoid daydreaming, she threw herself into work. After all, Mallory would be off to college within months and two years later Jenn would leave the house. Caren would be happily abandoned. She planned to expand the office and hire an administrative assistant. Her husband, Sam, claimed there was no need. He could barely shield his transparent lust for money and never would fully escape his mercenary needs. Forever insisting that he could live without a "pile of money," he died young.

Sam drank and ate in binges. When a massive coronary took him at age fifty-three, no one blinked. Sam arrived at work early, left late, and, if he grew bored, found women and wine to suit him. Caren, three months after his death, had modified her work ethic. She was still attentive but left the building early enough to exercise, relax, and share meals with her blossoming daughters.

Mingling with Sam's Jewish friends for twenty years had nearly converted her. She felt Jewish at this point, and despite her natural and then treated strawberry blond locks, most strangers assumed she was a Jew. Morris had been one of Sam's cronies. Morris liked Sam but could take the blowhard only in small doses.

They watched NFL football together, ordered in heavyweight title bouts on pay per view, ate bags of chips, and drank six packs of Miller in wholesale quantities. Now, with Sam gone, Morris wanted to help Caren and the girls. Morris did not have cash to spread around. He thought, somehow, Caren might like to help him get a storefront. While she had barely been involved with the business, Morris knew, from conversations with Sam, that when Caren had been even marginally involved in the business, she was on solid ground. Morris had to admit, no question on this, she was quite a catch.

Morris, Mendel, and Zena met Caren in the small commercial district east of the park. at ten that morning. She immediately showcased a place with separate entrances and connecting doorways. It took on the appearance of one store.

"Not bad. How much?" asked Mendel, skirting small talk.

"As a package, maybe $600,000 to buy. You won't find a neater buy north of Hartford. You can't do better there or even up in Amherst. This is it and a prime location, what with renovation plans in the works here," she said.

"Meaning," Mendel responded shrewdly, "I could do better in Springfield, maybe, with a little initiative."

Zena leaned into Morris's ear and whispered, "Mo, tell him to go easy."

"Look, there's no reason why she should fib," said Morris to Mendel, taking the smaller man by the elbow and twisting. "Caren, how about a single to show us? Or, could we possibly get just one of these?"

"Well, if you want to know," she said in that Yiddish chant which sounded phony, "there is one just down the block for a hundred grand but it's not much. Small? Of course. And the lighting is from hunger."

Mendel cut in, "We can install some lights. What kind of space you talking? Twenty-five by fifty?"

"The printout makes it seem more like twenty by twenty-five." She looked from one man to the other. "If I were you, I would stay here. Better in the long run without a doubt. Take the other and you're stuck – with no possibility for expansion."

"Listen, let me talk with my partner," said Mendel, suddenly assertive when it came to spending a buck. He yanked Morris to the side. "Listen, this broad, and she is one piece of work, ahem, don't know from nothing. We can get that space for two hundred, maybe less, but not from her. Tell her to bide her time while we mull over the offer."

"Caren, we need a few days. That's a lot of money."

"You don't want to see anything else?"

At once diplomatic and courteous, Morris quickly said, "Why not? We have time."

She drove them away to a small place several blocks away. They then went downtown to see a few storefronts. Caren pointed to the newly opened Basketball Hall of Fame, visible across the highway, and the hotel nearby. She claimed the city was alive with tourist trade – which could only help bolster Morris's business. But, the men weren't interested, having already seen the prime spot – near the park that they hoped to land.

Caren couldn't come close to selling at her price. She didn't see Mendel for what he was, a quick-fix gambler. She bargained conservatively while Mendel, as he whispered into Morris's ear, wanted "to shoot the wad."

Zena, nearly forgotten, spoke up as they turned up the hill toward Forest Park. "Mrs. Sussman, I don't know you. Just woman to woman, though, let me advise you that these boys have great interest and some cash to invest. Your lack of flexibility, your high price, is driving them away. Come down and you'll find yourself a buyer. Be reasonable."

"Zena!" cautioned Morris.

"No, maybe the ladies can settle this better than us," said Mendel, changing his tone while patting his friend's big belly.

Caren Sussman, just learning the real estate business, was sharp enough to follow a lead. "Yes, I will drop the men off at Mr. Kahn's house, then, Mrs., Mrs...."

"Lewis," Mendel and Morris chimed in at once.

"Yes, Mrs. Lewis and I will go off somewhere to talk this out. Is that all right with everyone in this car?"

Zena forced a smile as Morris and Mendel exchanged quizzical glances. Caren, driving away and simultaneously sizing up Zena Lewis, meandered through the park before entering Longmeadow, the wealthy suburb that abutted the park's southern edge. Within moments she had parked on the circular drive leading to a splendorous twelve-room house.

"You don't mind being my guest, do you?" asked Caren.

"Well, no, especially since they haven't taken me to this lovely, little town."

"It is clean. More pleasant than living in the city and safer, I might add," said Caren, forcing a sigh to elicit sympathy. "I do miss Sam. If only he didn't drive himself to death. We had a lot going for us."

"I'm so sorry," said Zena.

"Don't be. This, what's happened, pushed me out of the house and up on my feet. They even ache less. I like business, enjoy pushing. It is lovely, though, when I'm home. My children are grown, at least nearly. Do you have any of your own?"

"What I have in my life you see before you. Correction: I have my sister, Gilda. Sometimes, I think I have Mo. But, that's far from settled."

"You from New York?" asked Caren. "After 2001, I dread bringing it up."

"Florida. Mo and I met at a shuffleboard tournament."

"Now, I remember it all. I read about you, the ladies team you organized. Someone wrote it up for the JCC Newsletter, whatever they call it these days." Caren paused. "Now, what do you think those boys will really pay for those stores?"

"What? You actually have no interest in them. It's true. You only want a profit."

"Answer, please," said Caren. "Of course, I'm concerned about them. Why not?"

"These men are trying, late in life, to live out a dream: a café and a shop mostly for older people. Not those in your age group, not for early or middle mid-life. We want seventy something and over, like me. It was all Morris's idea."

"I didn't know," said Caren, whose self-assured, smug tone revealed that, really, she did know. "I suppose we can sell it for maybe under two hundred and still turn something. No lower," she advised.

"With mortgage rates high again, they can't carry such a loan. Be realistic, be sympathetic, one, the other, or both, Mrs. Sussman. Give me a figure we can work with."

"One fifty is lowball, the word I was told to use."

"If that is it, I will go and tell them."

"I don't want to lose the sale. If they can't pay, maybe I can go to someone above me and they'll work with it. I would think not, but who knows?"

"Fair enough. Drive me back so I can present this to the men."

Caren Sussman was an involuntary hair twirler, equally proficient with either hand. Shoving Zena into her seasoned Mercedes, she twisted one of her rear locks toward the front of her head. Caren, who knew she couldn't possibly get much out of her passenger, very much wanted to get rid of Zena, and without delay. Nor did she find Morris, the fat one, enticing. Caren knew that the scrawny looking one had some cash. When she got him alone, she would pump him, hook him...whatever seemed necessary. Caren didn't know much about business but she was blatantly greedy. She dropped Zena by the front walk and abruptly said good-bye. Zena noted the real estate woman's negative attitude and transformed demeanor. Zena trudged forward with the knowledge that she had failed in her mission.

Suddenly, she called back, over her shoulder, turning her neck to view Caren. "I didn't mean to put you off by bargaining."

"No problem, long day ahead of me. We'll be in touch." Caren's smile was forced and, as she turned toward the road, her lips neatly zipped back into place.

Feeling the weight of her age, Zena plodded into the house. She called for Mo, then for Mendel. No one answered. Odd that the place was deserted. Morris had told her they would be awaiting her return. She looked in Mo's closet. He had left behind his orthopedic shoes in exchange for seldom-used New Balance walkers. His ancient gold sweater, with the umbrella on the chest, was missing. He had taken a hat, one with accumulated dust.

Mendel needed something for his head and the old fishing cap always did the trick. Zena knew just where they'd gone. After a few sips of orange juice, she began the half-mile trek across the park. Compensating for her earlier disappointment, she held her posture, feeling light, even proud.

She found the M&M Boys gorging themselves on hot dogs, French fries, and soda fountain cokes. Next to egg creams, cola of any sort, Coke, Pepsi, and unheard of brands, too, were Morris's favorite drinks. An addict, he drank cans and bottles as others chain-smoked cigarettes. Kiley and Ted Shawn sat next to the boys. Soon, Zena came into view.

"It's your Fraulein," said Shawn to Morris.

"Anything but that is the case. You, my friend, are absolutely incorrect. You never met anyone so anti-Fascist in your life. Even somewhat anti-German she is, which does not comfort me," he added. "Now, what with this new millennium and the crazy media spins, she doesn't trust a thing she reads," said Morris. "No one is so paranoid of Germans."

"Except her sister," piped up Mendel. "Gilda will not ride even in a German car."

"Same genes but probably not same jeans," quipped Shawn but only he laughed.

"That woman is a peach, and some player, too, I might say," chimed in Kiley, fastidious and color-coordinated as ever. He adjusted his stylish Ralph Lauren button down shirt and pulled his sleeveless sweater up over his head. "Hello!" he called. "Nice to see you again."

Zena was anything but pleased to be there. She scolded all the men and narrowed her gaze upon Morris. "This is something, Big Mo. You leave me with this shyster realtor and go off for fun and games."

"She's not Jewish, Zena. She just acts the part," said Morris.

"I am the one, nevertheless, trying to bring the diva down on the price of the storefronts while you two are outside playing games, like you're twelve years old."

"Morris, she's right. I am up here so I might as well get involved in this deal," said Mendel. "You want to open a store, you need a place? Correct me if I'm wrong."

"No argument on that one. You claimed, just the other week when we spoke, that you would not budge an inch until we showed you something."

"Nu? I've changed my mind. Something less than two hundred thousand and it sounds like a deal to me. Let's get this business moving, so we don't spend the weekend bogged down in real estate connivings."

Morris shrugged his shoulders, looked straight at Zena who smiled and nodded. It took him no time to ready papers. Mendel quickly signed an agreement to put up half the dough just as soon as the combatants arrived at the precise figure. Having bought and sold for years, he considered himself a seasoned pro. This was his turf and he knew he could expedite the process.

Caren Sussman had not conducted such a major transaction. Though she had the proper forms on hand, she was not quite certain of the process. Instead, she twirled her hair, and, to her horror, actually pulled out a few thin strands.

***

Soon enough, it was Sunday afternoon. Prior to Mendel's departure for Long Island, the resurrected duo sat around in Morris's living room. Zena had gone off by herself for a walk. This made Morris uncomfortable but he had grown to accept her ways.

"So, Morris, look at us. A few simple games of shuffleboard and here we are."

"Your meaning?"

""Friends for life and now, almost instantly, business partners."

"I don't follow."

"We are forming a partnership on the store. You don't expect that I am the principal donor without getting a half share in the business, do you?"

"What, I ask for a loan and get a partner I don't need? This is not my kind of deal and I have news for you -- I don't want a cheater and a crook like you."

Mendel spread his arms as if parting the waters. "Morris, calm yourself. You run the business while I, back with my sweetheart on Long Island, get my money's worth."

"No way in this world of corrupted values that I am beholden to you, Mendel. You'll be nagging all the time. Even when nothing is at stake, you're a gnat. I can hear it now. 'Why didn't you move those canes and walkers? Must you serve snacks at such a discount?' Those sorts of things."

"Be reasonable, Morris. You run your store. Whatever you make, we split. Without me, without my money, you got no store. You got no choice in the matter."

Morris seethed. "You are one dirty, slimy, little rat, Mendel. You told me none of this until this moment -- after we signed all those papers which I, dumbbell, did not previously read. I trusted you – you, of all people."

"This is a men's store. I kept the girls out of it, at bay, away from you, Morris. Zena, that woman of yours, she's some hawk. I couldn't get away with much, what with her snooping. The important thing, Morris, is that we'll be in the money, the two of us."

"Ha!" yelled Morris.

But within an hour, he had calmed sufficiently enough to see the point. If, God forbid, the store failed, it wouldn't be only his shirt that would be lost. Though Morris had seen the shop as his baby, Zena advised him otherwise.

"That skin and bones friend of yours, sharp as a tack, smart as a whip," she said, mixing clichés.

Having made her pronouncement, Zena went straight to the tub for a bath, taking with her a favorite chamomile soap. Morris opened the door just a crack to mention that he was off to the airport with Mendel. He did not pause to explicate the intricacies of the business negotiations. Morris, himself, needed further clarification.

As they neared the airport, Mendel began to squirm. It was his way of prepping for departure. "I will see you in a month and then what a surprise I shall have for you," he said. "In the meantime, the big check should arrive next week, and then you will be able to fix and furnish to your heart's content. It was good to see you, Morris."

Welling tears formed involuntarily and blurred the big man's vision. Morris covered his eyes with a large, red bandana and then softly hugged Mendel, his very best friend.

CHAPTER 7

Mendel had left his home address, phone number, and seldom utilized email address for Lucy that day he had departed the Holiday Inn in Virginia. He convinced himself that he rarely thought of her since. Meanwhile, the revitalized hotel chain was opening inns in Boston, Hartford, and in Port Washington on Long Island. Lucy was given a choice of locations where she could assume management duties at a branch hotel. Thinking that a small New England city might make a match, she chose Hartford.

When she arrived on site, she called Mendel immediately, having safely stowed his information in her purse. The building renovations had been completed but the hotel had not yet opened for business. Lucy dialed Mendel's number in Springfield but was given a forward to a Long Island listing.

"Sugar, this is Lucy."

"No fooling around. I only know one Lucy and she's not calling me. You, my sweet, must have the wrong number," said Mendel.

"And I am that sweetie. From the motel. You were with your big Teddy bear type friend, that big man, until you met me."

Mendel, stunned, did not utter a word. Finally, he whispered, "I cannot talk just now. You see, I have another woman here. I'm sure you understand. I mean I have a wife."

"I don't believe you," said Lucy. "Where are you anyway? Exactly how far from me?"

"I can't discuss it," said Mendel, cupping his hand over his mouth and the phone, too. "Leave me your number and I'll get back – when I can," he added.

Lucy was scheduled to be in the area for a week. With heightened airline security operative, she might find herself delayed before flying down south to get her belongings. She smiled inwardly, then blew a kiss into her cell phone as she closed it, placed it in its case and dropped the phone into her satchel.

Three nights later, Mendel fetched Lucy's number, extracting the crumpled piece of paper shoved beneath his stack of underwear, set deep in a bureau drawer. He could not make out his writing and was unable to recall the area code for greater Hartford. At one time, it was 203. But, they had changed it to 960 or was it 860? He chose the latter and dialed the number.

A man's voice answered in softened declaration: "Hartford Holiday Inn."

"I am looking for a girl, well maybe a youngish woman. Her name is Lucy and she is one of your clerks," said Mendel.

"I am not that girl. I'm the only clerk," said the voice from beyond.

"Hey, wise guy, she called me three nights ago. She might have that one-day flu or worse. She's got some terrific shape. Red hair, no freckles in key places," said Mendel. "She said she was in training. Even before, she looked like it – aerobics, whatever they do these days."

"You mean Lucinda, not Lucy."

"She told me Lucy. Either way, you know her?"

"Yeah, what of it? You her father?"

"I am sorry, Mr. Clerk. But, I am calling long distance. Is she there or not?"

"She went back down south. They decided to go with a man instead for this particular job. Me."

"What will she do, a pretty little thing counting on the position. What do you think she'll do?"

"She your kid or something?" the voice asked. "She's one strong filly," he said.

Mendel began to recover. He breathed deeply, like they said to in the senior yoga class Gilda once dragged him to. "Yes, a daughter/father thing, yes. Rather, a father/daughter arrangement would perfectly describe us." He paused. "You don't have any idea how I can reach her, do you?"

"Try Holiday in Richmond. Use the 1-800 so's you can chat."

Mendel grabbed at the phone and stopped, realizing the implications of such a call. It could, potentially, jeopardize all the good in his life – everything Gilda meant to him. On the other hand, he mused, then smiled before snatching the receiver.

In no time, he had her on the line. "Lucy, a wild goose chase is what I'm on, courtesy you."

"Sugar, you found me. And here I was, ready with a big, juicy surprise. They wanted me to go to the deep South but I asked for Northeast, just hoping to be near you. They just decided on a medium sized Holiday in a place called Manhasset. That wouldn't be anywhere near you?"

"Christ, but a twenty or twenty-five minute drive. What, in God's name, do I tell Gilda?"

"Who's she?"

"Someone decent and nice to me. This is a shuffleboard colleague, a teammate, someone I've played the doubles game with. Solid person, good friend." He paused. "Listen, sweet pea, I can't go for someone like you, what are you twenty-four or something. You don't want me anyway. I'm a scarecrow on the way out. I got some cash, yeah, I'll send you some."

Hey, sugar, I could snuggle up to some tall, fair, handsome CEO or even a ladder jumper. I like you better. We had a nice time that day," she said.

"Without a doubt. Listen, if that job is real, still call me. If not, nice being in touch again." He left her holding her phone.

***

Mendel concluded, as weeks flew by, that his life chapter entitled "Lucy" was not fully past tense. But, he had heard nothing more from her. What if she had forgotten him? Then again, maybe she wanted to call and was afraid. No, that was out of character. He was glad to be rid of her but exasperated and upset. How could this be? He decided to call her once again.

"Course I am still here in Richmond and I don't suppose I'll be seein' you for some time," she said. "They've decided to keep me here for a while longer."

Mendel spoke without considering implications. "I have a good plan, one I hope you will take seriously. So, listen to me. I could come up, again, to see my friend Morris in Springfield. He would welcome me with open arms. Maybe you could find your way to the Hartford hotel?"

"According to you, just a stretch back, I was after your money – period."

"Let's not talk. You just try to work this out in the next two, three weeks. The question is how to be in touch and the answer is I now have email. I will send you notes every so often and you say yes or no. In case you don't know, Hartford is not far from Springfield."

For the next several days, Mendel hobbled often to the computer he and Gilda had situated in their newly closed-in porch. Neither used the machine all that often. Still, Mendel worried that Gilda might find a strange email and put two and two together. Mendel had instructed Lucy to use an alias. He would immediately delete her messages after reading them. Nevertheless, he was nervous.

Mendel called her.

"I didn't email because that seemed such a stupid idea. After all, we're not all about jumpin' in the hay now, are we?"

"Please tell me yes or no," said Mendel.

"Yes. I went down on my knees, practically, to convince them to try me out just once more as a manager. I been a hostess down here, doin' all includin' servin' up cocktails. Not for me. They don't know how smart I am," she said. "Anyway, I believe, just to get rid of me, they're sendin' me back up to Hartford."

"I got a problem of my own. My Gilda insists she come along when I go back north. Last time I went to Springfield, she stayed here on Long Island and it wasn't her cup of tea. Now, she won't take no for an answer. So, I am taking her. When I'm there, when you're there, I will call you. At the hotel, so be waiting."

Gilda insisted that she and Mendel drive the Mercedes to Springfield. She now loved the car and leapt at the opportunity for highway driving. Gilda took the wheel for much of the trip while Mendel kvetched. The glare from the sun bothered him, his seat would not recline fully, even soft rock and roll on the radio antagonized him. It was a miracle, he thought, to doze on and off.

Mendel was driving the last leg of the trip when they passed the Hartford Holiday Inn, well-lit, just off the interstate. He squirmed, fidgeted, and accelerated hard, giving Gilda a start. She smiled but thought nothing of his antics, except that they were typical of this man whom she adored.

***

Zena and Gilda had been a tightly-knit unit for many years. To an outsider, it might have seemed unlikely that each could survive without the other. The women, though, kept separate lives.

Gilda, always angular, grew gaunt as she aged, at least until recently. Her acidic stomach having finally settled and calmed, she put on a few pounds. She also became more forgiving.

For decades Zena stowed her emotional self beneath a veneer of extroverted and sometimes agitated behavior. Zena had always turned to Gilda, the big sister, during difficult times. Whether it be their parents, male callers, or the vicious world, Zena sought out Gilda to make it all better. Zena was now seventy-five and another side of her character began to emerge. Gilda, for her part, missed her little sister but was glad for the distance. A couple of months apart allowed for confirmation of their mutual affection. Constant companionship tended to blur or even dash their friendship.

The women now anticipated a joyous, deep-felt reunion.

It occurred on an Indian summer mid-October day. Just beyond peak foliage time in New England, the temperature (Mendel citing global warming) surged upward in the eighties. Just a few days earlier brittle leaves had dulled slightly from resplendent red, orange, and yellow to more faded copper and rust. They crackled and crumbled when plucked.

Zena and Gilda hugged, held hands as they walked along the bike trail toward the hub of the park. It was a likely place to be, the grand park now reinvigorated, looking chic as it welcomed a wide spectrum of people, varying in age, class, and skin color. Zena steered her sister to the shuffleboard courts. Gilda, deliberate, drank deeply in the glory of the bucolic, urban scene.

"This is some palace, this park, Zena. Not like anything in Florida," said Gilda.

"Mo says it's a crying shame compared to what he calls 'the old days." Maybe, with this, he lives in the past. They used to have lions, elephants, deer herds, white polar bears, and some exotic birds. People in the neighborhoods were kept up all night what with roars and howls."

"Just think! You believe even part of that. He must be making it up as he goes along. Such stories."

Zena bristled. "I am not some naïve kid. Always the little one, that's what you still think of me, no? I got news for you. They have pictures in the downtown library. Go find out for yourself. You never trust me, Gilda, and you never have. It's not like I'm eight years old."

Gilda looked away. "It's not what you think, Zena." Gilda paused and breathed deeply. "Well, take me to your new, beloved shuffleboard courts. Twice only, since we came to Long Island, have I played. And those times with Mendel. On the Island, that's what everyone calls it, ladies our age just sit and play cards, maybe a little bridge. The active ones golf but usually only pitch and putt. And you?"

"The challenge match, which you know of, I'm sure. I, myself, practiced to play and coached the girls like it is a hobby. Otherwise, no, I don't play nearly every day. With my weight, no matter how I watch what I eat, I need a routine. Otherwise...." She patted her soft, rolling belly.

"I have eyes but, listen, you always go up and down. With Morris eating like a horse, too, it's no wonder you're not bigger. He takes three or four bites and offers you one. Am I wrong? In my opinion, you look good."

Zena laughed. "The two of us, Gilda, we know each other too well. Truth, though, is that Mo likes me on the plump side."

"I'm glad of that," said Gilda.

They held hands as they walked to the court. Never had one of their arguments, from start to finish, including cooling off period, lasted more than an hour.

"Who are those players?" whispered Gilda.

"The fancy-Dan one, that's Kiley; this other one with the yarmulke, that's Avram. The other two I have seen but I don't know their names. Most of the regulars are usually not here until a while later. We get a full house by three or four. Mo says they play earlier, with the sun as a heater, as it gets colder. This is a sign of age for sure: adjusting court time according to the sun's rays. Go figure."

Kiley bowed and Avram removed his yarmulkah while the rest stood at a distance. By now, though, the sisters, having joshed one another sufficiently, sought more time with one another.

"Let's walk to that small brick house," said Zena. "We can get coffee or Cokes." Gilda was glad to follow.

They sat in the corner of the shabby, rectangular room, beneath a black and white photograph of Carl Yastrzemski. A powerful looking young man stood behind the bar, eager to serve anybody, thankful to stave off the endless boredom of his daily routine. His headphones stuck to his skull as he dipped and bopped to music. He shared the space behind the counter with a sweet-faced companion, a young woman wearing a tight tank top with spaghetti straps. She must have sewn on her jeans. She watched as her friend waved to welcome the older women. All the while, he kept his headset on.

Gilda nodded. Zena parted her lips as if to smile.

"So Gilda, how has it been? A serious thing for you, this Mendel?" asked Zena.

"I don't know the answer. Mendel is a crab, a constant nag, a man who, no matter what you give him, is never satisfied. Not a good word for anyone. But, I like him very much. More with each passing day. And you?"

"Mo is totally impossible. He will not listen. If God himself appeared, he would not get a word in edgewise with Mo. Me, though, I am happier than in years." She hesitated. "All the time with you? Yes, these have been special times in my life. But, it's just different for me to have a man and all that goes with it. You know, Gilda?"

Her sister was already nodding before Zena completed the thought. "Maybe they are not the most handsome fish in the sea, if you know what I mean. Then again, at this point, neither are we," Gilda said, laughing.

"I'm pretty sure they consider us prize catches, Gilda. Never mind these lines on our faces or little pouches around our sides. After what happened what is it four years ago, at least we're all here. Let's be thankful. I don't even care that Morris can't touch his toes," Zena added, trying to keep a straight face. She looked around to be sure no one was within earshot before going on. "Gilda, it's been so long since I've been with a man, I am not so sure what I'm supposed to do."

"Oh yeah?"

"Sometimes I'm sure that I talk too much, so I cut back. Then, you know him, he's booming, taking up all the space. You and me, we know each other, love and hate doesn't matter. We've always been stuck together, like pea pods, since we were little. Living with Mo is different. Like I said, I cannot remember what to do."

"For me, dear little sister, to be completely honest, it is not what but who, as a woman, even as an old woman I am trying to be. Mendel keeps saying, 'No pressure, no pressure, sex is not in my top five,' but I know better. Mostly, he is terrified of death. He wants so much that I will be with him when he goes. That's when he's finally honest. Otherwise, he covers up by bragging about his conquests in bed. And some of them quite recent, from what I can gather. None of that really shields what's bothering him. You understand that, Zena?"

" Let's face it," said Zena. " I'm no Elizabeth Taylor and he's no Richard Burton – not in their prime, I mean. I sometimes feel a little uneasy about spending every night in the same room with him. After all, how long do I know him? Yes, he takes care of me and I do like him. He is so bulky and awkward that I get uneasy. Just a lot of man, in every way." Zena blushed. " I hope it's alright, what I'm doing."

Gilda quickly slid her chair next to her sister's, and, with her long reach, massaged Zena's yielding back and shoulders. "You always worried too much. You got a cold, you thought you couldn't go outside. You had a date, you were sure he would be ugly. If you get somebody good at this point, take it, take him. Don't drive yourself sick trying to analyze it again and again and again."

"My smart and caring big sister, I need to ask you a question. Is it too late in life to think marriage?"

"You two are moving along with speed faster than light, I would say. Think about the business first. Tying a knot so late in life, why not? Pleasure counts, too."

"I feel like I, like we are just starting out," said Zena. "Well, maybe this is fifty years or so late, but what am I to do? And the pressure of the clock, like a bomb about to explode, ticks behind us. I don't want to know only from helping guide his electric cart in assisted living. That seems to be the only hallway so many of us find these days."

"Mendel, on the other hand, tells me nothing is forever, never is it permanent," said Gilda. "I think he just feels any day might be his last, that one day he will wake up, keel over, and, in his phrase, 'curtains.' You ask him though and no chance that he would admit any reluctance to marry me – on the spot."

"Gilda, we've been away a good hour. Probably we ought to end this and get back."

"I should listen to my little sis more often. Still, even if we're here together only a short time more, we have to carve out a portion of life for just talking – like sisters. Correct me if I'm wrong but it helps?"

Zena nodded, grinned, looked into and through Gilda's still soulful eyes which Zena thought ran a deeper shade of green each year.

MENDEL AND MORRIS

***

Morris and Mendel had not spoken seriously with one another for too long. Now they drank heartily --- chilled glasses of Chilean Merlot while staring at an ancient television Morris had resurrected by another old friend. He liked this TV and the new, fancy one. A different television for different programs and occasions. The repairman was a Springfield local who, as a boy, fixed TVs and made quite a bit of cash under the table. Decades later, in retirement, he did the same and took the stash to begin a separate account. This cash he wagered regularly at a dog track.

The boys had it established that on upcoming Saturday they would inspect the building, half-plastered walls and all. Mendel agreed that by evening he would commit to the project or, at the very least, state his intentions and involvement. Mendel asked if, on the following Sunday, he could be left alone. He could not possibly reveal his motive – to call Lucy.

Morris and Mendel awakened early the next morning and tiptoed away, leaving Zena and Gilda, rooms apart, snoring loudly. The day was crisp and frosty and the boys were eager to walk a quick mile to the storefronts. The idea was to visit the place immediately, then go to breakfast where they would swap thoughts.

"There she be and what thinkest thee? Not one or two, but three beauties!" said Morris, obviously pleased with the buildings and with his language.

"Eh? I don't know. Almost always, this area has been a run-down mess, not your upscale locale, shall I say. Really Morris, you couldn't have done better than this? You could not have done any worse," Mendel said, answering his own rhetorical question before his outraged friend could muster a response.

Finally, Morris grabbed Mendel by the elbow before exploding. "You know what this city is like. What did you expect, the Taj Mahal, Scarsdale, or that Chappaqua where the Clintons, so I read, live? Besides, you were with me when we bought this," he roared.

Mendel could not quite break free of Morris's grip. "Okay already, let's go inside," said Mendel, shrugging and struggling simultaneously.

Morris reddened at his friend's feigned insolence and fumbled with keys before settling on one he thought might be a master.

"Come on, Morris, I got better things to do."

"Mendel, you just make things that much worse. You don't have eyes that are able to see how irritated I am? Jesus Christ!" At last, he found the proper key and after a frustrating yank and several jiggles, managed to unlock the door.

"You, Mr. Know-It-All, have to get yourself a locksmith and not just a bum. Get him to change all locks. Besides, that one is no good. It jams."

"Just once, stop your nagging, or I will squash you like a gnat."

The interior was shabby, dilapidated. Morris kicked at flaky plaster all over the floor. He detested the wall color, a sickly shade of green and brown. Morris felt as if everything might crumble at once. Fortunately, he had paid some high school boys to strip clean one wall down to the original brick. Mendel, despite himself, actually admired the result. Still, he looked away, hoping to conceal a positive reaction.

Suddenly he said, "Now that I like. I will give you all the credit. Not that this is anything new. Even on Long Island, which is not exactly Beacon Hill or Brooklyn Heights, they're going to exposed brick. Still, this is some snazzy look – as opposed to the rest."

"Follow in my footsteps, difficult as that may be for you, Mendel. Try, just for once, not to damn something you praise. This room, here, we'll make into our gift shop. We will stock items but also have places, comfortable couches and chairs so that people can sit and snooze. No hard benches and wooden seats, believe me. We want this to be as good as home…."

"Yeah, okay, let's see the rest," said Mendel.

" For now, we got to go outside to get inside, you catch me? Later, we will construct connecting doors." He brought Mendel back outside. Again, Morris could not locate the key to match the particular lock. Mendel squashed the urge to sarcastically mimic him, put him down with a quick jab. Eventually, they found their way into the next section.

"This, da dum, will be the lounge. Again, nothing even vaguely stiff to sit on. Here is a scale model they made for me: tables will be wooden – some round, some square. These cushioned chairs will be complete with arm and foot rests. Recliners, too, no need to worry. The racks of magazines and newspapers will be replenished each day. The Internet people will have ports so they can get online, something I am finally learning about. For those who wish to remain pleasingly plump, we will serve an array of Danishes, coffee, tea, maybe even espresso."

"Now, you're cooking, percolating, whatever. It might have taken you too long but, Morris, this is the best idea you've had since I know you. Don't stop there. Why not open a small coffee shop? You, we got the space."

But Morris could not read his friend. Was this a snide retort or a genuine compliment? He played it safe. "I don't know about that. Number one, where would I start and number two, where do I get the cash to kick this thing off?"

Mendel straightened his back and shoulders. "For this maybe I could be even more helpful." He looked his friend squarely in the eye. "I have wanted, since I was a young man, to have a café."

"And now, you live on Long Island, the leading strip of land in this country for bowling alleys and two-bit restaurants. Not exactly South Beach, this schmaltzy palace everyone raved about when we were in Florida."

"You don't need to worry where I live. Just show me more."

Morris walked his friend through a labyrinth, in one door and out the next before finally leading Mendel into the third component.

"Call a lawyer and, once again, sue me but I don't know what we do with this one," said Morris.

"My money helped buy this thing."

"We'll come up with something good, maybe a game room," added Morris.

"You goof, you. Put in a couple side-by-side shuffleboard courts, run yourself a little tourney when the joint opens, you got it made."

Morris raised his bushy eyebrows, one black, one silver. "Not your worst thought by a long shot. But, we're talking more money. That's not to mention zoning, always the enemy."

"Shush, we come up with the dough, we do it, and make more back, even if we are not at our very best. Zoning, shmoning."

"To breakfast," Morris declared.

"When your brain cells clog, you always, I mean every single time turn the talk to a meal, snacks, the convenience store...."

"Maybe my brain functions more cleanly when my belly is full." He patted his protruding paunch.

"Not likely but this is you, the Morris I know so well."

The boys ambled to a remodeled shack which advertised eggs, toast, home fries, and coffee for a buck and a half.

"Oh, so they drop some rotten food on people like us, poor, unsuspecting victims. It's low this price, but what you get is probably a sick stomach."

"I am here five days a week," Morris lied, "and as their most loyal customer, let me vouch for these eggs, right off the farm." He was fibbing and Mendel knew it.

By the time they were on their second cup of coffee, Mendel conceded the food to be "passable for hick country." Morris was thinking of business. "This partnership may get somewhere – that is, if we can make it through till the fall."

"Partnership, my golden dome, this is my cash that you use for fuel! What you talking?" Mendel screamed, neck veins popping.

"Excuse me, sir, but, in this case, u is part of us, if you get the point. In case you forgot, this is our store. Zena and I are co-managers. Yes, you are loaning us capital."

"Without me, Morris, you got no store. You and she, maybe just she will run the business I am funding. My dough, my business. If anyone's got brains, it's Zena."

Morris, advised to count to ten when he had once suffered what he termed a "phantom heart attack," tried to breathe deeply. He downed half a cup of scalding black coffee. By now, everyone in the restaurant was watching. "We can work out the details at home." With two hands, he lifted the astonished Mendel off his stool. Now," he said, "Let's go. I, as in I, will pay the check." That accomplished, Morris shoved Mendel out the door.

***

Next morning, Mendel awakening before sunrise, rushed to get on the road to Hartford before the onslaught of commuters. He left a note saying that an old business partner had called, "a fiscal maven who could offer them sound advice. This guy knows concepts, the difference between a pipe dream and what works, so I thought I would try out the indoor shuffleboard station bit on him. Sayonara, Mend."

"That man of yours, he can't think straight sometimes but when he writes he is golden. He makes more sense on the page. I dunno." Morris held Mendel's morning message a good two feet from his eyes to make it out. "He turns phrases, as those intellectuals say. Or, am I wrong? Maybe we could call him a journalist."

"He is up to no, no good. That's what I say," said Gilda. "He didn't mention any old buddy of his in Hartford. I don't like it."

"Look, don't worry. His looks, yes, they deceive. You think he's falling apart, but he's healthier than most."

"Maybe that's right. On the other hand, he thinks he can control anything and anybody. I say this is bad news."

"My sister needs to obsess. Always, she's been this way," added Zena.

Mendel, meanwhile, had left Hartford proper in search of a small village just to the west. Questioning anyone he could spot and track down, he had determined, at last, that the Inn, while listed under

Hartford in the phone book, actually split the West Hartford/Farmington border. He knew little of such towns.

Still, Mendel's sense of direction had always been reasonably keen and he accelerated quickly, speeding toward the Holiday Inn, which he located within minutes. Arriving, he straightened his back and walked forthrightly to the reception desk where he asked for "Miss Lucy Rayman or whatever her last name is."

"Never heard of a such a person," said a visibly irritated night clerk, bleary-eyed and in need of sleep. "Describe her."

Mendel gestured, then spoke, "Curvy and lanky but so well-built, if you get my message. With bright red hair, long and thick. Wavy, too."

"Well, the cocktail waitress here is named Lucy and she has red hair but it's dark, like almost brown. Tightly curled, auburn head of hair, I would say. What's it matter to you, Pop?" he asked, squinting at Mendel.

"I'm her Uncle Menford, here on family business, from the Springfield area. Could you direct me to her, please?"

"Asleep, like I should be," he said. "I imagine she's sacked out on a couch since she's been working the lounge 'til two in the morning on weekends. Otherwise, she made it to her room."

"And where is that?"

"Without no authorization, as far as I go, it's none of your business."

"I am here," Mendel lied, "to tell her that she just came into some money. My brother Horace just died and he left her some change. Furthermore, the store Horace and I opened is now making a small profit – even in these times of stock disasters, foreign wars, scandals and so forth. I want to share some of the money with my favorite niece. Now take that, Mr. Investigator. And whose business is none of that? That would be you," said Mendel, poking the man in the bony chest. "Be more helpful and kindly point me in the direction of her room."

The man's attitude changed immediately when he sniffed that something might be in it for him, even a tip. "Yes, sir, it's the fourth one on the right after the hall bends just a bit." Mendel nodded appreciatively.

"Only," the clerk added, "she might have company. With Louise that wouldn't be the first time."

Mendel understood perfectly but made no acknowledgment. He marched stiffly but purposefully down the corridor and knocked three times just above the number plate announcing Room 104. No response.

"Lucy!" he called, remembering to throw his voice. "It's me, Mendel." He heard a rustle of covers and the muffled sound of hushed voices. Someone quickly came to the door.

It opened wide and she stood motionless, wearing a crimson robe with white piping, revealing the wide, pale chasm between her breasts, now half covered with gauze-like cotton fabric. Mendel immediately realized she was naked except for the thin garment. She smiled sweetly and Mendel thought she had a scent of honey. But, she did not usher him in.

"I am so, so tickled to see you," she said, shaking her head and working the corners of her mouth as if she had just awakened. "What a shock, what a surprise," she said, but didn't seem particularly startled. Lucy made her way into the corridor where Mendel held his ground. "I never thought you would call," she said, again without a trace of feeling but with a more evident drawl. She reached back to shut the door of the room she'd left.

"If this is the wrong or an awkward moment, I can come back later, another time even," said Mendel.

"You might call it a bit of a strain, but not in the way you, sweetheart, might think," she said, clearing her eyes and throat.

"The night clerk, who is tipsy as a drunk, told me you might be entertaining," said Mendel.

"What a horror! What nerve!" said Lucy. "Not true. Just that something else is in there with me."

"Out with it girl. If I get stood up, it won't be the first time and probably not the last."

"Come on in and I'll give you a good view," she said as Mendel wiped sweat off his head with the back of his hand.

She yanked him in by the shirt collar, reached beneath her bed, and produced two white, yipping, curly-haired poodles, one with a baby blue bow around its collar, the other sporting a plaid vest.

A startled Mendel lurched backward as the dressed-up pet jumped him. The dog sprinted hard at him, squealing and barking at the cornered Mendel. Covering his face with a handkerchief, Mendel stumbled out of the room, slamming the door behind him. A moment later, Lucy, flushed and smiling, appeared.

Wafting her fingers before her reddened cheeks, she panted at him. "I'm so sorry. Bonnie, the blue one, is just fine. But her big brother, Dabney, he's been sick goin' on a week. A terror he is, especially when he has a cold."

"I notice." Mendel also saw that Lucy was passionate about her dogs but simply polite to him. Such a wholesome sight she was that Mendel could easily forgive her. After all, he had been stringing her along.

"You know, I'm allergic to dogs, all kinds. Any dog and cats, too, for that matter."

"Men, I didn't have any idea," she said. "I'm so, so sorry."

He found her irresistible. "Scrumptious," he whispered to himself but she reacted as if she had heard.

He suddenly took her in his arms, all of this in the open corridor, and felt the pressure of her full, warm breasts upon his spindly chest. She collapsed against him, and he felt her as she wedged firmly against his shirt. To his great astonishment, Mendel was aroused. "Maybe," he said, "allergy won't be such a problem."

"Sugar, give me ten minutes to freshen and get ready. Then, we'll get some coffee and breakfast for you. Nothing too fattening for me," she said, sucking in more than a hint of belly he did not recall from months before. Lucy walked away, leaving a grinning Mendel, who by now had grown quite rigid.

Twenty minutes later, Mendel, aggravated and fatigued, walked slowly back toward the front foyer and sat opposite the night clerk, who, completing his shift, was tidying papers.

"She is something I, unfortunately, will never experience," said the man at the desk.

Mendel wasn't sure if he was meant to hear that pronouncement.

"Is it really true that "the piece" is your niece?" asked the short-witted clerk.

"Oh, she is, but more than that," replied Mendel, delighted to taunt the fellow.

"Just once in her pants, that would be all I would ask."

"Why should you worry ? You got plenty of years. Well, at least until they blasted into those two towers, I thought so. Me, for sure, my time is running out. On the other hand, now, more than ever, what is that saying, make the most of it? Follow me? You got some chutzpah to talk about Lucy in that tone of voice. Listen to some advice from an old man: If you want to get somewhere in this world, be a son of a bitch but only if you need to. Not many people understand what polite means these days. I used to think playing by the rules would get you somewhere. No more. Not with women and it won't get you rich fast either. I was brought up to obey The Ten Commandments, may my parents rest in peace. If it was important to pay attention, I would. Being kind to everyone, where did that get me? Nowhere. It wasn't until after the second big war, when I started breaking other people's balls instead of my own that I made my way."

The graceless clerk said, "Here comes the lady," as his eyes bugged out. "Feast your ancient pupils on this."

Lucy came strolling down the hall wearing a low-cut turquoise leotard, matching stockings, and a blinding red velvet jacket lined with a strip of fur adorning the collar. Mendel slapped his thigh. The quick sting assured him that he wasn't dreaming.

She had smeared on aqua eyeliner and pitch-black mascara which had begun to drip. Her blanched face provided high dramatic contrast with her plush, crimson lips. She had evidently doused herself with pungent perfume though Mendel did not recognize the fragrance. Forgetting his arthritis, Mendel walked fluidly around the room, his formerly throbbing shoulder now pain-free. He needed to be tip-top for this girl.

"Caught her, huh Pop? You got something to talk about for the ages right there," said the night clerk.

"Not to worry. You'll get your share, Bud," said Mendel, hooking the arm of this exquisite prize with his own. He followed as she led him toward the dining area. Mendel looked back and winked at the incredulous young man.

Lucy snagged a couple of menus while en route to the table. As they sat, she leaned directly into Mendel and deposited a full, wet kiss on his forehead. "Those puppies embarrass me so," she said, slowly running her tongue along her dewy, glistening lips.

"I'm fine," he said. "I won't let nothing bother me. Let's talk," he said.

Lucy, shifting her demeanor, was instantly reserved. Mendel, anticipating a hearty appetite, found himself picking, nibbling at his food. Where was the flirt he had met during the summer? He pushed his eggs about, broke his toast apart, but ate little. Lucy made short work of her full stack of buttermilk pancakes.

"What, dear Lucy, has this dirty city air done to your spirits?" he asked. "You eat okay but you do not seem all that interested in me."

"I am perfectly fine," she said. "Sugar, am I acting a little stiff?"

"You're acting like no one else is here with you, my sweet. I might as well be back in Springfield or Long Island or even in my grave, head first." Mendel, when nervous, would often resort to morbid humor if at a loss for words.

"Well, I am just the slightest bit confused by this situation."

"Yes, Miss Rayman."

"Lucy Redmond," she corrected.

"Whatever your name is, just blurt it out. The jig might just be up. What is your game?"

"Another, a different man."

"I somehow assumed you wouldn't wait forever – for me, a fragile geezer," he said.

"Uh huh. But, he is another daddy, like you," she paused. "I mean another older man. He might have seen his last days in a gym but he is there to take care of me -- sometimes."

"You mean you spend time in bed with him, is that it?"

"Not so much that. He just likes to be with me. Same as you. Takes me places. You know men. They cotton to be with girls who are still firm, like me. Makes them feel back in their prime, I guess," she sighed. "Treats me like I'm the Princess Diana or something. Buys me nice, shiny things. I get some kind of doll treatment, I tell you."

Mendel, outraged, tried to shield his reaction. "You consider me and this King of Siam or whatever to be in the same boat as far as you are concerned?"

"Not exactly, Mendy. I actually like you better. It just seems to me that he doesn't have anyone else. Maybe you do? I didn't want to tell you about him until now when you asked. Anyway, this has only been going on since I came up here. So, it might end tomorrow, for all I know. Right now, he's back in the city on business. He owns one of those big insurance companies. Was a trader until the bombings but luckily out on vacation when the towers went down. His company now is located more in the center of Manhattan, that's what he tells me. I don't really understand. Not that we talk about it very often."

"Enough. I don't need to hear anymore about this. I'm a disgrace. If Morris or Gilda or her bossy sister, Zena, even heard about this, they would be wise to deposit me and my belongings on the street. I don't know what got into me to come here." With that, he shoved his plate in front of him. "Enough of this, Miss Lucy or Louise Redford!"

"Redmond and it is Lucy."

"I got to get away." He stumbled out of the dining room and crossed the main entrance of the inn. The clerk happened to be out in the parking lot, having completed his long shift at the desk.

"Need a lift? Something wrong, Mister – can I help you?"

"I got no use for you. I'm sorry, it's not your fault. I made a big mistake," said Mendel, fumbling for his Mercedes keys and covering his eyes to camouflage welling tears from full view. "It's my own damn fault," he croaked as the young man waved to him.

CHAPTER 8

Although she initially kept her observations to herself, Gilda noticed some changes in Mendel as they drove home to Long Island: He was certainly more compliant and peaceful as he inched closer to her in the front seat when she took the steering wheel. He made small talk, the type of chatter he rarely initiated in the past. Then, Mendel became quiet, as if sinking into himself. Gilda began to fret.

"Mendel, what's wrong? What's the matter? Nothing you have to complain about?"

"I made a promise to myself when they blew up the Trade Centers. Unless I got a sore on my skin which won't go away, Gilda, please be quiet. I admit, at first, I didn't keep my own word. Now, though, you want me to let you in on everything that bothers me? I can't please you nohow?"

"It's just that it isn't like you to ignore maniacs who pose as drivers here on the highway. Something must be eating away at you."

"What if you got it right?"

"Tell me, I can't stand the suspense," said Gilda.

He cranked at his cheek with his left hand. "My lips are zipped."

Gilda could not pry them open. Mendel remained silent as he drove home, too quickly and quietly to suit her. They remained subdued throughout the ride and as Mendel took an exit off Southern State Parkway. He took the short cut he was certain was exclusively his own discovery. Gilda could not imagine living, even in relative silence, with this man.

At first, however, she tried to pretend that all was well. Gilda returned to routine activities including bridge night, two mornings at the health club, the Jewish Women's Book and Study Group. Mendel sat and read about the Civil War, cleaned the house twice a week, once more than necessary. Gilda observed Mendel closely, watching him age perceptibly from week to week. He looked as if he might keel over at any moment. This, of course, is precisely what he had been claiming for many years.

Gilda prepared a special pot roast dinner the following Sunday, but Mendel did not seem interested or eager to partake. Suddenly, he half lifted himself from the dinner table, looked at her directly, and said, "Gilda, I miss Morris. Life without Morris is, you might say it's just too easy for me. You make it smooth, no problems."

"That is what I do wrong? Furthermore, that is what you been stewing about all week, Mendel?"

"Not only that. While I was in the dump or at the swap shop, I concluded that maybe I need my best friend back. Maybe that would make a difference." He paused a beat. "I want you, too, Gilda. It isn't what you may think."

"Ok, so?"

"I can't live here anymore."

"And me?"

"That's your decision. If I have some say, you're coming with me."

"You want me, you want it that way?"

"I am nothing if not a stubborn, crotchety old man. I can be a burden, in case you didn't know."

"All of a sudden this one is worried about other people way too much. He's on the other side of being concerned. If someone would have told me this a while ago, well that would have been some laugh."

"It strikes me," said Mendel, "that I can't be all that much fun to be with, live with." He was thinking of Lucy....

"I came North with you because I wanted to be with this ornery grump of a person. You're not quite the bum and such a bad time you say you are. A little obstinate at times, yes, but...."

"Like you're a dreamboat yourself? What do you mean?" he asked.

"Mendel, at times your head is swollen, not so much that you're full of yourself but that you listen only to yourself."

"You got me confused with Morris. I refuse to be associated with that bullheaded buffoon."

"Whatever you say, but you just told me he was the one, that absent link in your chain. Now that you're starting to sound like the old Mendel, God forbid, what is it that you next have in mind for us?" Catching her breath, she asked, "And where?"

"The only place where I can have both you and Morris – the City of Homes. And you can have your sister back, what's more. What do you think? Of Springfield?"

"Of my sister, I used to be more certain. As long as I don't have to live with her, that's fine. I won't complain about it. I can't deny that she is, well, we are a part of one another." She held up her wrinkled hands, "Back and forth, both palms. Keeping some distance, though, will help me to like her even more."

"So we'll move. And you will manage not to make me feel guilty. After all, I'm dragging you, shlepping you there."

She sighed, "I will try, cross my heart, to be the passive little woman if that's what you want." Gilda sounded resigned rather than enthusiastic.

"You know," said Mendel, "this house never did agree with me. I bought it, maybe fifteen or seventeen years ago when I could steal it off the real estate market. I don't know what I paid – cannot even guess. And the absentee landlord business has been good for me. Except, deep down, it never made me comfortable, renting to someone else."

"You made your small fortune, and you still have a nest egg. Such a shrewd businessman I have found. Who knew?"

"That's different. Selling furs is one thing but charging a lot of money to live in your house, that's another. Anyway, it is time to unload. I'm too old to manage. And this island, so called, filled with gas stations and bowling alleys and movie theaters, that's fine for some. When I want classical, I go to the city. Live there or live in the woods or in some cottage by the ocean. Not this. It doesn't suit me one bit."

"That's all there is to it?" asked Gilda.

"Enough for now. I've said plenty."

"We'll pack in the morning. But, I want to enjoy this roast which took me all day to prepare."

Mendel wedged himself into the chair, his favorite one since it allowed him to slump as it conformed to his shape. "I would like to say only this to you, Gilda. Thank you."

***

Mendel and Morris lived on opposite sides of the expansive, well-traveled park. That much of a physical separation was fortunate and had probably helped them sidestep many a quarrel. Mendel had purchased his duplex with the intent of leasing the upper floor. Shortly after, the grace period for the previous owner's tenants expired. Mendel quickly asked them to move out. Uncomfortable in the role of evil landlord, he helped them find a new home with similar space. Mendel craved square footage. He never had any intention of either renting the upper story or expanding his quarters. Every so often, he wondered why he ever made the acquisition.

Now, returning to Springfield, he would precede his furniture, most of which he had temporarily left behind on Long Island. He allowed realtors to sell the Nassau County house far below cost. He hoped he might get $300,000 but would settle for less. Soon enough, the moving truck arrived and Mendel, surprising himself, asked that anything extra be placed in the vacant upstairs rooms. There it stayed while Mendel and Gilda prepared themselves to resume life, as a couple, in Forest Park Heights.

Twice a week, Mendel and Gilda would eat dinner with Morris and Zena, each twosome alternating as hosts. The men fell into a familiar rhythm by supervising the storefront renewal while the women organized shuffleboard, then a table tennis program at the JCC. Morris and Mendel, visibly delighted to see one another, soon began to bicker. Such contentiousness proved to be a cornerstone of friendship.

By mid-November, the walls and ceilings of the stores began to shine. Only the floors needed further sanding and polishing. M&M began to think of furnishings. As ever, they were at odds. Morris wanted "only the best, top-notch stuff." But Mendel insisted that they first search Goodwill and Salvation Army for second hand goods.

The week before Thanksgiving, a blizzard hit the area and dumped fifteen inches of snow on Springfield. Morris had procrastinated roofing until the deal on the shops fell fully into place. Now, the decision to wait came back to haunt him. A portion of one ceiling suddenly collapsed, leaving a huge leak where adjoining walls for two store sections met. The heavy snow began to snake down into the wall and Morris panicked that the excessive water might ruin the recent plaster job. Mendel faulted Morris, rather than the weather. Morris was outraged.

"Shmuck, you couldn't fix the roof right away? What's wrong with that pea in your head you call a brain?"

"Don't use that language with me, Mendel. I can still crush you with one smack from this fist."

"Why must you leave what needs mending today until, always, I mean always, tomorrow? Didn't your Midwestern mother teach you such a simple rule?"

"First, you leave her out of it. Second, Mr. Moneybags, if you weren't so goddamned tight with a buck, I might have had the whole roof redone on time. But no, I'm watching your cash. That's what we're paying for now. Meanwhile, we are taking a major soaking and I'm not trying to be funny. And leave my mother out of this."

As they spoke, water seeped into unknown crannies. Morris proclaimed that the damage would be incidental and insisted they wait out the night and the storm before patching the roof. Mendel had other ideas. That evening, directly after dinner, he complimented and complained to Gilda that her brisket of beef "was like nothing I have ever tasted in my life." Stuffed to the brim, he needed to walk off the meal. Mendel put on a pair of old galoshes well past prime usage, pulled his furry Cossack hat over his bald head down to his eyebrows, and bundled himself up in his stadium coat. He tied a threadbare muffler around his neck and plunged forward.

Much to his surprise, Mendel's legs served as strong anchors as he trudged through the snow beneath him. Never, though, did he reach ground level, however mightily he pushed downward. Mendel wondered if this is what astronauts felt as they floated about in space. He yanked the scarf across his wrinkled face as the biting wind whipped from behind and then around him. He walked in what he hoped was a straight line directly toward his new store.

Mendel had carefully pocketed each of three keys in case any doors or locks had frozen stiff. He was surprised when he was able to walk through the front entrance which was not blocked with snow. He grew furious that the heat was pouring through the ancient steam radiators. He swore at the utility company for eating his dollars before they had opened for business. Morris had helped Mendel drag in two ancient but still functional standing lamps from the top floor of the two-family. Mendel yanked them into the center of the room and watched as water drizzled slowly down from the ceiling (still lacking fixtures) to the dividing wall. Mendel remembered that the work crew used an aluminum ladder and was able to locate it at the back of the third room. He yanked at his coat pockets and drew forth caulking and sealing materials, gunk to stem the tide. He carried insulation and tape from his own house. Mendel thought none of this would work but why not try to stop the leaks? Damned if he was going to let a freak snowstorm ruin the enterprise, and waste the money he had put up front.

Slowly, pausing at each rung and stopping frequently, Mendel began to climb the ladder. A stabbing pain in the back of his left thigh bolted upward on an angle to the small of his back. Mendel thought he was paralyzed. He tried to snap the leg straight, which heightened the stunning cramp. He whispered to himself, "This is what it feels like to be shot."

"Oy!" he cried, just once. Never did he wish to be seen as an old Jewish man. He tried to keep the Yiddish he had mastered as a child to himself. This was different and he involuntarily shrieked again and again. It was beyond his control. Suffering a complete loss of equilibrium, he toppled over and fell to the floor, clutching the back of his bent, crooked limb. When his right leg went out on him, Mendel, in disbelief and woozy from the pain, lay motionless – too exhausted, even, to scream.

Never had he experienced such extreme torture. Alone and fearful that he might freeze before someone found him, Mendel recalled that time when, as a boy, he cramped up while playing broom handle stickball in the city. That feeling, however, departed as quickly as it came upon him. Now he sat, crumpled from the waist up, dislocated from the pelvis down, frightened to his bones. He could not shake his legs free and the harder he tried, the more they contorted. No one could possibly find him. No phone had been installed and he didn't know from cell phones. Mendel visualized his body rotting away.

Despite the throbbing beat of a certain torn muscle, he slithered like a worm along the splintered floor until he reached the front window. The hard gobs behind his knees drilled through him. Mendel knew what he had to do. He grabbed a straw broom, half-clinging, half-dragging, and limped away. At the base of the window, he rested, coiled and contracted into an asymmetrical ball.

He hoped that by banging as hard as possible on the glass he might draw some attention. Everyone else, however, was safely home. Who else would be roaming the streets on such a night? After smacking the broom against the pane for what seemed to him an hour, he sank back down, wheezing, resigned that he would simply die the most undignified of deaths. Unless he stood, no one could see him.

Mendel realized he had to make a commotion in order to attract someone's attention. To do so, though, he would have to elevate himself which, at this point, he could not manage. From a sitting position, he slammed the weighty brush against the window five, six times. Thud after thud. He could only hope the percussive eruption would work. One final smack might save his skin. Mendel drew the stick back and, with a mighty swoop and a shriek to match, he shattered the glass which splashed about the sidewalk, the interior, his body, head, and clothing – a shower of shards and triangles strewn indiscriminately all over. "My arteries," he said with renewed voice, "I have cut through and through. I'm a goner." The frigid air rushed in while Mendel remained quite alert, assuming the worst.

Still unable to straighten his legs, he collapsed into a crescent shape on the floor and felt himself drifting off....

It seemed to Mendel that just a moment or so had passed before a siren blast battered his brain. He looked up to discover policemen and firemen surrounding him on all sides. A man wearing a red and blue plaid flannel shirt was holding smelling salts beneath Mendel's nostrils.

"Don't worry. You're okay, you aren't dying. You're slightly in shock. I'm just making certain you will fully revive. Dr. Kay is my name," said the man who looked, to Mendel, like a ringer for Santa Claus.

Mendel responded by lifting himself up ever so deliberately as he pieced together the puzzle. "Listen, I am Mendel Greenbaum. This is my store. Last night, I had these unbelievable cramps in both my legs. Was it like this when those towers fell? I wish I would stop talking about that. All I could see was glass and then I don't remember a thing. Now, a whole crew of people is here. Where's Gilda? And Morris and Zena?"

"Hold on, Mr. Greenbaum. You evidently broke the storefront window with the push broom and when somebody in the doughnut shop heard the crash, he came running and found you here – out cold. Do you recall any of that?"

"Well, I remember thinking I would have to raise some kind of hell or else kaput, that's the end of me. I guess, I mean I cannot deny hitting the window, but it's my property. You can't touch me on that one."

McKay's potbelly shook as he laughed. He gently cradled Mendel's head in his arm. "No, Mr. Greenbaum, no charges against you, that's not why we are here. Of course, you have to replace the window, but that's up to you. Now, I don't want you struggling to get your footing. That is not a singularly wise idea. Tell me though," he said, with a sudden and serious tone, "are you in any kind of pain at this moment – whatsoever?"

"Pain, rain, shmain. I am always in pain, don't you doubt that. Nothing worse than the usual. The backs of my legs, that's different. They kill."

Dr. McKay massaged, then gently manipulated the limbs, caring for them as if they were delicate as those belonging to young children. Inching the right leg to a nearly ninety degree angle, he questioned Mendel. "Hurt here? Here? What about this side?" He repeated the procedure several times upon each leg until he was quite satisfied that Mendel could now support his weight.

"Mendel, you've had problems walking lately? You haven't been eating well?"

"Gilda, she feeds me like there's no tomorrow. She can cook a roast in a pan, covered or not, like nothing you've never seen. No, in answer to both of your questions."

"Well, your legs cramped up for some reason and it's often a chemical imbalance. Possibly a vitamin deficiency or even severe stress. Do you have a history of spasms or cramps?"

"No. Everything else, yes. Until now, no cramping."

"And what about anxiety in your life?"

"This farshtinkener roof is what causes a pain in my rear and every other place," he said. "That much I can tell you."

"Pardon me, I don't know that word."

"Forget about it but big, fat Morris, my partner, did not have the roof fixed when he should have. If I ever see him again, not even one of his excuses will I accept. Look at it leak! See with your own eyes."

McKay began to talk to himself. "You're a lucky man, Mr. Greenbaum, that you were found alive soon after you went down. Not that you would have suffered permanent injury, but you would be in far worse shape than you're in at this very moment." The doctor, his watery eyes reddening, did not smile. He pursed his lips together when he spoke, as if to form words before uttering actual sounds.

"Well," said Mendel, "I'm going to die soon enough, so what does it matter?" He shrugged his bony shoulders.

"What concerns me is your health at this moment," said the terse McKay, barely opening his thin lips this time. "I suggest that you schedule an appointment at my office next week. I'll leave a card after we've called your contact people." The doctor grew more perturbed with each passing moment.

"Now, you listen to me, young man. I am going to try to stand, to go vertical as I have heard young kids say these days. Or, is this a bad idea?" He paused. "You understand what it means to patronize, no?"

"You could help yourself in the future, Mr. Greenbaum, by applying a warm compress and some wash cloths before you stretch out. These spasms come on, leave abruptly, return without notice. If you grab onto my forearms, I will help lift you to an upright position."

Mendel hoisted himself to his feet bone by bone, then limb by limb, clinging to the physician's shoulder. There was a sudden commotion outside the door. Mendel knew that only one man was capable of creating such a racket.

"Mendel, Mendela!" roared Morris. Gilda and Zena followed. "We came as soon as we heard. But, we could not drive nor walk – there was no way to get anyone else. We called a cab driven by a meshugge driver who nearly rammed into a pole. Mendel, you don't look so bad, at least considering. What's new?"

Mendel swiveled to look at Dr. McKay. "You see what I got to contend with in this business? My partner. I am the one who was stuck smack in the middle of that long white tunnel, staring death down. He is the hysterical one. Listen, you nogoodnik. This, this is Dr. McKay, my savior. McKay, let me introduce Morris Kahn, and Zena and Gilda Lewis, athletes par excellence."

"Folks, this is the best, the strongest, the most spirited he has sounded," said McKay. "He must be glad to have his people with him. Are you all family?"

"That we won't answer because it isn't clear, maybe even to us," said Zena. "But, if you ask whether we are all closest of friends, you've hit that nail right on the head."

What became of the traumatic event, though, was nothing. Within two days, Mendel assigned the recent, unfortunate incident its significance as something of the past, and resumed life as his normal if dyspeptic self. He and Morris argued often without ever reaching resolution. Nothing had changed. They always disagreed. The Lewis sisters were no better. Using one another as sounding boards or foils, they chattered incessantly as they reviewed, to the point of exhaustion, the trail each had taken to Springfield.

It was with great relief, then, that they decided to share Thanksgiving together. The tasty, stuffed bird would surely serve as a unifying catalyst. The house was, for a short time, complaint-free. Zena and Gilda, without even a momentary bicker, assumed duties in the kitchen. They began to prepare while Morris and Mendel went to the grocery store and bought cranberry sauce, rolls, and canned gravy.

It dawned on Morris that this would be his fourth traditional Thanksgiving since the world had changed. Just two months after nine eleven, he and Mendel were at a local tournament, maybe in Worcester. They had dinner on the road, in Sturbridge, to make it special. Both men felt isolated and without family; neither mentioned it.

Morris considered Thanksgiving to be his holiday. That said, he and Mendel spent the early afternoon bickering with one another, collectively damning the shabby job the Ackerman Brothers had done with the roof at the store. The old men glared at one another, continued to snipe and banter -- about nothing in particular. Forgetting their history, they filled the air with personal insult.

Having accomplished nothing that afternoon, the boys eagerly anticipated the party. They left the store and shuffled towards home at a snail's pace, as if each of their steps might be a final one.

"Beaver!" yelled Mendel, with alacrity, as they turned a corner.

"What is this you're talking about?" asked Morris.

"You can still hear, you dumb ox. I said Beaver!" screamed Mendel once again. "And there's another one, over there!"

"So, I haven't lost hearing in both my ears. What, pray tell, as I once read in some Shakespeare play, is the beaver?"

"It already passed us – a red wagon, foreign," said Mendel.

"Listen, I would tell you what a beaver is but I don't want to be disrespectful." Morris looked around to be sure no one was within earshot. "You look up a woman's dress, you got a beaver."

"Beaver!" shrieked Mendel, once again.

"Shut up. I don't want any part of your dirty mind," said a scowling Morris, his face curling up like wet potato chips.

"No matter. I'm in the lead, with two beavers to your none."

"Mendel, I see no crotches. I don't see even one furry, little animal. Of course, we might have to go back to a pond in the park, which is not reasonable on such a day as this. Where is this beaver, Mendel?"

Mendel dug an elbow into Morris's belly. "In the country, I regret, they never taught you this game. You decide upon a certain car, color and model. You look for it on the road. Whoever spots it first yells beaver. That's how you play. Even someone so simple as you should follow. The truth, Morris, is that you are one deprived man. Your youth in cow country did you wrong." Mendel's deep breath caused his entire frame to shake. "I forgot about this game for, what, thirty or forty years. Until I met up with," he gulped and then burped, "Duke Snider, in Florida."

"Sure you did, Mendel. Why and how did you happen to become good friends with Duke Shneider?"

"Not Shneider and not Jewish," said Mendel. "I'm talking Snider, of the bums in Brooklyn. I met him early one morning as Gilda and I were driving north. She was snoring -- sawing up something awful, so soundly was she asleep. I left her in the car for a minute to get a coffee-to-go from a restaurant. There he was about to get into his car and drive away when I recognized him. I stopped him and we struck up an instant friendship. Before I knew it, he was driving both Gilda and me out to the Dodgers' minor league park. I got to watch, first hand, those kids just learning how to play baseball. And the Duke, too."

"Let's say I believe just a small fraction of this, Mendel. What is with that beaver game?"

"So, I had forgotten all about it until Duke Snider, himself, suggested we play it as we drove. Imagine that. Mendel Greenbaum and Duke Snider playing beaver in Vero Beach, Florida. That is something I would never have believed, never wagered one penny on it even if you gave me great odds."

"Mendel, I don't know," said Morris, but the big man had taken the bait. Morris swallowed every bit of Mendel's fib.

The men walked home in silence, each wondering if the other retained even a shred of credibility.

The women, meanwhile, busied themselves preparing food and cleaning house. It was easier to serve the meal in Morris's place with its extra room. The men wanted to watch television on a large, flat screen. Mendel was very much perturbed, however secretly, that his brand new Sony could not compete with Morris's machine. Since when did Toshiba go one up on Sony? Mendel wanted the latest, the greatest brand.

Zena and Gilda were pleased to reacquaint. Sharing apartments for years, they had come to take one another for granted. The recent months of separation served to draw them together and they felt genuinely heartened to find time for girl talk all to themselves.

Hilton Lewis, their father, had amassed a fortune through textiles. He had worked in a mill as a teenager and, like Horatio Alger – that is what he told them - worked his way up the corporate ladder. Before he died, Lewis owned several mills and wisely liquefied a large portion of his asset income to provide capital to last his daughters through their lifetimes. He had the perception to invest long term, too. He wanted, for his daughters, what his parents never experienced – fiscal security.

As a young woman, Zena managed an office for a small insurance company. Gilda had set her sights upon teaching in an elementary school, but found herself, instead, reading copy. She worked for advertising agencies and publishing houses. A meticulous woman, patient with detail, she never attained her degree and did not complete course work which would have enabled her to teach little children. Nor did Zena finish college. When their father passed away during Eisenhower's golden early 1950s, the women packed their bags and made off for South Florida.

There were suitors. Zena, before packing on pounds in middle-age, was   handsomely endowed and alluring. Gilda, on the other hand, never would have made it as a sweater girl. Always fit but flat-chested, she compensated with quick wit and barbed tongue. Anatomical opposites, the sisters remained close. Their once intense sibling competition disappeared with passing years.

While otherwise lolling about in soothing Florida sunshine, spoiled silly through their inheritance, the women, for some time, were, from time to time, unemployed. Each would take a part-time job. Zena and Gilda, lacking the motivation and urgency to work, never sustained professional careers. They preferred to retreat to a condo where they drew drapes around them as if creating a cocoon. Within the web of security, they withdrew from the workforce, relieved of the obligation to grapple with life's daily quandaries and struggles. They played shuffleboard often - until they met Mendel and Morris.

"Gilda, so what do you think of this Springfield of theirs?" asked Zena, as they hoisted the nineteen pound turkey on to the table for basting. Morris had insisted they purchase a bird no less than seventeen pounds, certainly sufficient for aging adults whose appetites, excepting Morris, had waned.

"Those two need each other. Probably they need us, too, but definitely they cannot live on without exchanging rude remarks. So dependent each is on the other."

"You're not answering my question."

"Do not, once again, put your cart before your horse, Zena. First, we must talk about combinations: Mendel, Morris, Zena, Gilda, whatever. Then, we can talk about Springfield, Chicago, Florida, whatnot."

"All right, Gilda. But, tell me something," implored Zena. "Didn't we have this conversation that day when you and Mendel drove up after the benefit shuffleboard match?"

"True enough, we started to talk then. But, I've got something more to say," said Gilda, fastening together ends of turkey bones. "I'm not so sure we're doing what is right. Here we are, maybe more than one thousand miles from home. We just picked ourselves up and left everything including a sister, some good friends, some not so good, all that was familiar and for what? Two meshuggeners."

"You wait, Gilda. I'm more than happy. I like this city. I involve myself in many activities here," said Zena.

"Go ahead, be personal, be defensive. But, if what you mean is organizing an old ladies' shuffleboard team at the Jewish Community Center, I got news for you. That's something, but not much."

"What's wrong with it?"

"If you plan to live the rest of your life circling around Morris and otherwise coaching decrepit biddies without coordination, well, that's fine. He's crazy as a loon, believe me, and will go off whenever he pleases. You realize he's doing this project only because Mendel gave him money."

"He loves me, Gilda. That's real and, after a lifetime of frustration, I will take it. You're the one to talk."

"I had my share of boyfriends when you were not even old enough to know," said Gilda, still the big sister.

"You're talking fifty, sixty years ago, Gilda. Tell me about the last five, even ten years. Tell me your stories and I will tell you mine."

Zena grew silent. She moved away from the turkey and bent down beneath the sink. Straightening, she showed Gilda a dark bottle.

"And just what is that?"

"This is whiskey. Would you like to join me?"

"Yes, dear Zena, I would," said Gilda, nodding. "It's not that I have a big problem living with Mendel, even under these circumstances. Back in Florida, though, I felt that I could go back, maybe, to college. Here, no. It's different. There, yes. Sure I love him. But, should I stay here?"

"Tough question? I don't think it really is. What's to stop you from taking classes here? From what I can see, everyone does it. Poppa left us plenty of money. Use some for that."

"It's not money that blocks me. It's the idea of doing something new, unfamiliar, getting out there. It's almost like dating. I used to be brave but now I'm all show and no action. Down there I know my way around and somehow feel more up to it. Here, it might take me years and who knows, given what is going on in this world, how many days, even, any of us has?" Gilda's voice began to crack and her eyes immediately filled with large tears.

"Gilda, Gilda, we are at the point, exactly, where we cannot put off until tomorrow...." Zena's voice waned as she held and sheltered Gilda. "You know. We need each other and, fight and scratch with and at each other as we do, we lean on each other's shoulder. After all, we're sisters. If you want my opinion or if you don't, I think each of us is better off only with these men. Where we live doesn't matter. No big deal. Hot weather or cold, we are both well into our seventies. You might say that your blood has thinned but your skin is thicker. I'm not buying that garbage. That would be kidding ourselves. We are just as sensitive as we used to be. We need more than just a man. All four of us, somehow, got to stay together."

Gilda, embarrassed to break down before her kid sister, began to compose herself. She dabbed at her cheeks, turned away and arranged her hair. "Talk about years. I haven't had a cry like this since I lost Isaac. That dog, second to you, Zena, meant so much. I feel better for this, what, shower of tears. Enough. Move on to the turkey. If we're going to eat before dark, into the oven it goes."

Zena put her lips next to the slick looking bird. "She never stops ordering me around," said Zena, speaking to the turkey while pointing at Gilda.

The men arrived home shortly after three, each surprisingly gracious. Gilda and Zena, eyeing one another, were taken off guard. "What's with you two?" asked Gilda. "I haven't seen such unified looks between the two of you since you dragged your tails off the shuffleboard court when we humiliated you in Florida."

"Never mind that minor loss," said Mendel. "It's about this business which we are one hundred percent positive will be one big, fat winner. Isn't that right, good buddy?"

A relaxed Morris nodded in agreement. "In fact, we are gonna make some killing," he added. "This is service and fun, too, so it all figures into a neat equation," he said, staring off into space.

Zena was suspicious. "Whether I've lived with you five months or fifty years, I know you. You are a constant pain, you know where, and you are forever pretending. Why now? What happened, today, Mo, which makes this the sure thing?"

"Should we tell them, Mendel?"

Mendel shrugged and slowly broke into a lopsided, sly grin which showed a dimple in his creased, cracked cheek. "A little bit of this, a little bit of that," he said and gestured toward Morris.

"Someone, a man named Paul Duranger, called us – even on this day. He's from Boston and represents a state-wide agency. It seems he's a friend of Kiley's, of all people, who advised him, as if Kiley is an authority, about our store. The state, no less, is interested." Morris raised a clenched fist above his head.

Mendel snapped his finger. "With this, a little financial support. Pumping up the

community may mean money for us, in the end, of course."

"You act like two little boys who just stole the cookie jar and found it filled with Mallomars," said Gilda.

"Something like this, a gift this big, we never expected," roared Morris. "There's this tiny nugget, too. If we are successful, maybe we could start a chain – open other places in different locations. Start with Worcester, Boston, some suburbs, and move on to Connecticut or Vermont, whatever."

"You live till you're almost eighty and then begin a pop and pop retailing business?" asked Gilda, displeased.

"Gilda, why must you be such a sour pickle? You, too, could benefit if this works out," said Mendel. "You would have something more to do than criticize everyone else."

"Excuse me for saying a word," she replied.

Morris plopped down on a couch, TV remote in hand. He began to channel surf, stopping, as was his habit, to watch commercials. Morris memorized little ditties to amuse himself.

"They must have something good," said Mendel. "Used to be Dallas against Chicago. What happened to Detroit and Green Bay?" he asked.

"Now, with digital, with Direct TV, with satellite and whatnot, you can get whatever you want. Back then, you couldn't even see past the snow on the screen. My side of the park, in the old days, always had better reception than yours. You have to admit this, Mendel."

Mendel, irritated, stayed in the kitchen. He fiddled with a place mat, picking out individual strands of fabric before Gilda slapped free his fingers.

"Shame on you. This was a Chanukah present just two years ago from Rebecca, my best cousin."

Mendel curtsied at the knee. "I am so sorry to both of you," he said, disingenuously. Zena and Gilda, as little girls, had learned the value of presentation. Their mother, a mediocre cook, took great pains with décor and color. She placed cloth napkins in distinctive holders, made certain that, on holidays, salt and pepper shakers were most distinctive. Her daughters followed suit. Trappings meant the world.

Two bottles of wine, one red and one white, graced the table. The vessels were swanlike and elegant. The large turkey, removed precisely to reveal its golden/brown exterior, was surrounded with: yams, cranberry sauce, Zena's special popovers, Gilda's French green beans glazed with ginger.....Mendel was stunned into silence. When he finally spoke, it was with a distant voice.

Morris, on the other hand, toasted not only the women and Mendel, but also the turkey, the occasion, and their new business. He slapped Mendel on the back, setting off a coughing fit.

Content to simply be there, Gilda rested and ate deliberately. Zena, in contrast, gobbled down two portions of white meat before attacking a drumstick. She sampled each side dish. Concerned that she might split her pants, given her tendency to gorge, Zena wore a neutral green shift, which neither flattered nor betrayed her swelling figure.

A day earlier, Morris purchased an entire rum cake from La Fiorentina, which he deemed the best downtown pastry shop. He and Zena polished off a few slices, while Mendel picked and poked at his. Gilda stuck a finger in Zena's side. "You'll blow up even further if you don't cut this out," she warned her younger, puffier sister.

Later rather than sooner, as the satisfying meal drew to a close, after even coffee and tea, Mendel rose and made his way to the hallway closet. Cradling a bottle of Courvoisier, he smiled wide and suggested cordials to cap the evening. Gilda, citing her doctor's advice, declined. Zena, patting her protruding stomach, tried to beg off. Morris, though, had left the table and returned to position a perfectly symmetrical goblet at each person's elbow. Mendel, dutifully following orders, meticulously poured each of them a desired amount. The ladies' cups contained a small portion of liqueur while Mendel filled to the brim chalices for Morris and himself.

Mendel raised his hand, bowed his head, and gestured to all. The four of them stood with him.

Shushing everyone, Mendel, looking like an ancient rickety tree which had seen more prolific days, slowly lifted his arms. He was atypically and gracefully calm when he spoke.

"You may have noticed, during this past meal, that I did not squint, squirm or even kvetch in the least. This, for me, is not so easy. These movements are like nervous tics. They comfort me." He looked up, as if delivering a formal address during which he was pausing to allow the words to settle in. His eyes sparkling clear, Mendel refocused, zeroing in on his subject matter. "This has been some handful of years. We found each other and lost, if not our best friends, then people so close to us. Yes, all of this when the trade buildings went down. We need each other now more than ever. This is true since we are not living until the next century, that much I know. I have a plan. It's been hatching in my brain for months and now is the time for birth. This has to do with where we all live. Maybe you will think I'm crazy as a loon or even just a head-in-the-clouds dreamer. This is no world for feeble old Jews on their way to nursing homes. We can't go to Israel, or even places like Idaho, God knows. They say to stay away from Paris."

Morris, waving his hands, began to erupt. Mendel, both of his palms facing toward the floor, signaled him to sit. "As I was saying, and I don't mean to be morbid or stupid, we cannot live forever. But, we can live together. So, whatever time we have left, we should make it the best – in each and every way. To get to my point, we should get our heads and what's left of our bodies under one roof – together. My place, which is two houses in one, will do the trick, I can tell you that. Young people, they try out all sorts of arrangements. Why not us? It does mean using stairs. So far, though, we can do it. More than that, you, Morris, and your lovely Zena, could use the exercise. Take the upper level, we'll take down. Dinner once or twice a week, at least together. What do you say?"

As everyone smiled, Mendel slowly sat down in his chair. Morris, grinning ear to ear, raised a glass in silent toast to his old friend. The women followed suit.

CHAPTER 9

No one was quite sure what to make of Mendel's notion. If they pursued it, what would follow -- gain or strain? Zena was most favorable, Gilda not so. Zena missed her older sister but Gilda could not imagine risking a good thing, her life with Mendel, an exclusive partnership. Morris tried to think in business terms and the economy was bad as it was. Morris, with Mendel under foot, would thrash and bash. How would that possibly help the new place? Could a working relationship withstand their friendship? On the other hand, maybe it would strengthen them further.

Morris wondered, too, where the women fit into the scheme. Would Gilda want a lasting involvement with the store? Zena, for sure, would then want in. Did he want the girls, with all their newfangled perceptions, constantly chiming in?

Gilda kept to herself, hatching strategy. A week after Thanksgiving, on a Saturday, as they sipped red wine, she divulged her plan. She had created a logo for the Forest Park stores: Phases I, II, and III. Simple but to the point. Everyone liked it. Minutes later, she and

Mendel sat in Phase II assessing space to use for maximum effectiveness. Years earlier, Gilda had actually taken architecture and planning courses. Besides, she had a sharp, intuitive eye. In this regard, Mendel trusted her fully. She kept shuffling ideas for tables, chairs, couches, and a full coffee counter. Each time she tossed a suggestion at Mendel for review, he modified or rejected it outright.

"Mendel," she complained, "you are more concerned with your grand vision than with us, with me. We are two women well past middle age in case you didn't notice or remember, and we are not used to men, especially codgers like you two. Who even knows if this dream, when push comes to shove, will work? We could be stuck here with nothing. Uprooted from Florida, bending our lifestyles to meet yours, and where does it get us? What, a commune or something? The four of us?"

An exasperated Mendel waved his arms like a stricken crane. She would not listen to him, number one, and, besides, no one could decide what to put in the café. "What, she thinks we're a bunch of nogoodniks?" He addressed the floor. Then, turning, "Is that really what you think of me and what I said? You don't know me better by now?"

"That is a real question. We know but do we truly know? We are all here and we are close. I am past, what, seventy-five and you say you don't believe it. Enough. How many changes in my lifetime must I withstand before cracking up entirely?" By now, Gilda was shouting.

"Just maybe you are onto something. Looking at it differently, this is a last chance for, I suppose, intimacy? It means less for us if you know what I mean. They move into my, into our house. We're the stable ones," Mendel said.

> Gilda asked, "You're trying to measure who gets fractured more by this arrangement?"
>
> "Gilda, no more twisting, please." Mendel stamped his foot nervously.

"Do you not see, with your still keen vision, that if anything happens, God forbid Morris or I am sick, even you or Zena, we then have a built-in to take care of one another? That is what we must live for. We no longer have families, we lose more friends each day. I, who vowed never to do so, read each day two sets of obit pages. It's a pity and it's the future. We must provide and protect. Excuse me for ranting on and on."

> "I see that," she said, tentatively.
>
> "But?"
>
> "I don't know if I can live in Springfield, and with more than one other person. I am used to my own room and maybe sharing a couple others but only with my sister, whom I have known forever."
>
> Mendel shrugged. "What could be better than this?" he asked.
>
> "Mendel, I am not saying no, nor yes. I need to think. I cannot swear on the Bible right now that this is my dream, too."
>
> "Okay, okay," he stammered, too perturbed to say more.

***

Zena, without notice, decided to diet. A day after Thanksgiving, she awakened and could not find one pair of pants which didn't cut her in half at what should have been her waist. Disgusted, she rifled through her wardrobe, cursing the clothes dryer ("No matter what you set the control, it shrinks everything!"). Finally, half dressed, she stood up in front of Morris, who was propped up against the headboard, supported by two pillows. He was snoozing, snoring, pretending to read the New York Times.

"What do you think? Am I just a few pounds over or very, very fat?"

"What a question to ask. Have I ever criticized your looks?"

"Answer now. Are these rolls (she grabbed the loose flesh around her middle) too much or can you live with them?"

"We all could stand to lose. End of discussion?"

Zena reached into the walk-in closet and emerged with a tent-like wrap-around skirt. "I am going on a crash diet," she announced. "Not only that, I am going to exercise, too."

"If you wish, suit yourself."

"You might consider it yourself. It doesn't do your heart any good with those folds of flab around it."

"What else is new? They been telling me this is true for years. And here I am, healthy as a horse."

"Except for falling on your face when you collapsed in Florida."

"Nothing but a fluke," he answered, nonplussed, staring into the newspaper.

"Fluke, shmuke, you're a fat old man and I am no lightweight neither. I am off to the mall to get hold of some warm-up clothing. That's what they wear, you know, these days, for exercising."

"And breakfast?"

"I will pass. If you had a brain, you yourself would skip it."

"This you call a diet? Starving yourself? Try Atkins or something instead."

"I ate enough on Thursday to last me the weekend."

"Zena, this sounds nuts, cuckoo, crazy. Next thing you'll be running around the park like kids half our age. Or on roller skates, complete with knee pads and a helmet. On an empty stomach no less."

"You come up with something better and I will consider it. Meanwhile, get your fat self out of bed or don't lecture me." Zena realized that she sounded too nasty – much more mean-spirited than she felt. She said, "I'll be back by noon," and walked away before regretting more of her words.

Morris slowly rose, then showered, shaved, and prepared some food for breakfast before leaving for the store. He and Mendel were to meet an architect/contractor at eleven o'clock to discuss plans for laying shuffleboard courts in Phase III. Morris had gulped down his chocolate Entenmann's. The doughnut sat like a chimney brick at the bottom of his stomach.

***

Each day something – snow, sleet, or freezing rain flew down from the sky. An old-fashioned winter gripped Springfield, home of the Basketball Hall of Fame, and its residents. People were forced to cancel trips and children missed school. Masses of snow dictated that travel plans alter. Everyone seemed stuck in place and irritable for lack of action. Morris and Mendel, working with one another on a daily basis, argued less and laughed more easily. Occasionally, they even compromised and forged intelligent business decisions. They saw relatively little of one another outside of the workplace. The couples led separate lives. Zena volunteered at the JCC and Gilda enrolled in an elementary education class at Springfield College.

Before dawn each morning, Zena was up and jogging through the park. She began with just a lap around the ball fields but, within a few weeks, she was covering more than a mile. She also began riding a stationary bike at the JCC where she worked out diligently. Not surprisingly, she lost a quick ten pounds and, before long, reduced her weight from a high of 170 to 140. All of which delighted her. She showed off by buying new, tighter outfits.

Gilda, physically passive, remained rail-thin. In fact, Mendel suggested she see a doctor. He did not let on that he feared she might be wasting away. Gilda would have none of his advice. She loved reading long-winded history books and essays and figured it was time to go back to school and, in old age, become the teacher she always wished she had been.

She imagined volunteering at a pre-school or becoming an elementary school aide. Why not share with the very young? Especially at a time when the world was threatened by bombs, hijackings, suicide missions. She could then be a teacher and help, even if just one person per month. Gilda thought hard and remembered the time decades earlier when so much seemed possible.

The sisters, shifting directions, scheduled a weekly lunch at the new downtown "Healthy Living" restaurant. On a particular Wednesday in mid-December, Gilda sat awaiting her sister, who was more than thirty minutes late. Zena was punctual to the extreme, always known for arriving absurdly early for engagements. Hence, Gilda was concerned.

Zena had slipped on an ice patch earlier in the morning. No one had thought to call Gilda who was most upset that she had not learned of the accident earlier. To track down her sister, Gilda called the Jewish Community Center and found that X-rays were being taken at a nearby facility. Thinking the worst, Gilda panicked. Fracturing a hip, at this stage of life, would be traumatic. Gilda trotted and slid through melting slush to her car. By that time, tears were streaming down her cheeks, she was terrified and saddened so.

The medical center staff attempted to divert her but Gilda, tongue moving swiftly and convincingly, talked her way into the X-ray room. There, she found her sister, in obvious pain, moaning. A dutiful nurse ushered Gilda from the room. Gilda was advised that this was not a life or death situation but that she needed to wait patiently for several moments. Gilda was directed back to an outer corridor where she sat, realizing that she had not yet said hello to her sister.

Nearly an hour later, the same nurse, now warm and apologetic, returned to find Gilda and led her through the hallways to a two-person room and Zena. The nurse informed Gilda that the hip had been broken and would be surgically repaired the following day. Fortunately, there wasn't any need for replacement and a full recovery was likely.

"Zena, I am so, so sorry. That I was not with you, that you are in such pain," said Gilda, tears welling anew in both her eyes.

"Don't fret. I feel like a fool, Gilda. Run two minute drills through snow and ice, then I slip on a sliver just when I'm heading in to shower. Ow!" she screamed.

"What is it?"

"Every inch of my body hurts. The painkiller, it doesn't do any good. Never have I felt anything like this, Gilda."

"You are so brave," said Gilda taking her sister's hand and holding it in both of hers. "Does Morris know?"

"No. He must be at the place with Mendel. It isn't like I've had any time to call and tell him what I've become."

"You look terrible," said Gilda.

"What can you expect?"

"I'm sorry, Zena. I can't think straight, seeing you like this. We never should have come to Springfield."

"Some other time, some other day, Gilda."

"When will they operate? Do you know?"

"Tomorrow if they can. The older doctor, who reminds me of my Uncle Herbie, may he rest, won't open his mouth. So, I asked the younger one, a little like cute John Travolta."

"You mean the old crotchety one won't tell you?"

"What can I do? He said they would have to take more X-rays and then decide if it was totally necessary. The young handsome one cut in and said it would almost surely be tomorrow." Zena paused. "How are you, Gilda?"

"Same as ever. I haven't gotten lunch yet, but.... "

"Okay, already, so I spoiled our date, too. Don't make me feel any worse," said Zena.

"Nonsense."

The head nurse, who hobbled badly, arrived with a tray for Zena. Gilda sidled over, eyeing the food. "Only for patients," explained the nurse, as she tried to coax Gilda out of the room.

"She's my sister and I am a close family member. Let go of me. Just a few minutes more with her is all I ask."

The nurse walked away, leaving Zena and Gilda, neither of whom had anything more to say to one another. Gilda was certain surgery would occur the next day and she was preoccupied with conveying the information to Mendel and Morris.

"I will be back later today," Gilda said.

"Gilda, I'm sorry. Thank you."

"Don't be foolish," said the elder sister.

***

A team of doctors operated upon Zena at eleven o'clock the following morning. The surgery, fortunately, amounted to little more than a routine fix it job. The prognostication was that Zena's hip would function well, that she, before too long, would begin to move about with some freedom. She looked forward to resuming shuffleboard activities.

Morris was far from at ease conversing with an ailing and subsequently recovering Zena. Those first days after surgery, Morris was all too quiet. He visited but didn't know what to say. Finally, as she mobilized, he began to speak.

"So, you feeling any better?" he asked.

"Better, yes. Good, no. What's going on with the store?"

"Catalogues arrive each day which means we're getting ready to order," he said matter-of-factly, without his sometime haughty innuendo.

"And the courts?"

"Coming along nicely. The café part, too."

"Mo, I'm still the same me. Zena. You didn't know that an old lady could possibly ever slip and hurt herself? What's with you?"

"I have never seen you look smaller, even the slightest bit helpless."

"Thank you for such concern, but I am not a basket case. On the other hand, the snap was like the wishbone from a chicken."

"You heard it break apart?"

"I was falling, falling, trying to balance, hoping to land on my behind and then," she hesitated, "I couldn't do nothing about it. Like skidding on the highway on a black piece of ice, you couldn't see, I only prayed to God that I could escape."

"So, Zena, is this so bad or not?" Morris asked, scrunching up his nose and cheeks. He hoped this would show his concern.

"I might have died. Some people go early. Look at that wave in Asia which killed thousands and thousands. But, I had surgery, which is risky to people, even for the healthiest of us at our age."

"You won't be doing so much jogging around the animals in the next week or so," said Morris, trying for a joke.

"That old goat of a doctor, he says never. The one who looks like he's still a boy, he tells me not to give up."

"And shuffleboard?" he asked.

"No problem. This is the phrase they all use. Anyway, shuffleboard, for me, is likely to happen. All of them think I will be more than okay to stand up, take a step, and fire away."

"Zena, you know, you don't look so bad, in terms of your color, at least."

"Nu? I don't feel tip-top terrific. I favor this hip, with the pins in it, and the rest of me aches. When you had the heart attack or strain, whatever you want to call it, what did you think, feel, and fear?"

"The end. Kaput. Death."

"You see?" gestured Zena.

"I see, crystal clear, exactly what you're talking."

MENDEL AND MORRIS

***

Zena set aside her cane three weeks later, just prior to the first night of Chanukah. The hospital nurse told Zena to use it for a month or so but she tossed it away a week ahead of schedule. The foursome gathered for a big meal, the first as a group since Thanksgiving.

Mendel insisted that he lead the service since Morris, "as a young boy, learned Hebrew backwards, with the wrong emphasis." At least, according to Mendel, this was so. Morris was not pleased, realizing that his own Hebrew accent, flat as a Midwest pancake, would become instant fodder the moment Mendel heard it. Morris had been coerced to study the language well beyond Bar Mitzvah, and he took pride that he had developed his own style. As he recited, he often gestured with his hands. Now, however, Morris mumbled under his breath as Mendel sang the blessings. Zena, vigorously rubbing her left side, remained silent. She sat awkwardly upon the special air cushion she had brought along. Gilda, thrilled to be preparing and cooking in her own kitchen, welcomed responsibility for the entire meal.

The meal, hearty though it was, did not achieve Gilda's expectations. Dessert was another story. To celebrate the occasion, Gilda brought out apple-raisin cake, with optional whipped cream and ice cream, both on the side. Mendel, trying his hand as the diplomat, put an index finger to his lips to shush everyone else.

"You got some kind of bug? You don't think free speech applies during meals?" asked Morris, jabbing Mendel with his elbow.

"It's not what you think. I have something to say to everyone. I mean each person in here should listen to me."

"Mr. Mendel Greenbaum is about to speak. Quiet in the house because, so help me, he must have earth-shattering news," said Morris, winking the same eye, in succession, at Zena and then Gilda.

"Maybe, I mean let's consider, again, merging these two families. We are all discovering that life is no less a struggle when you get to this point. We all got our fingers in the business. You have to admit we're best friends. Why not make it official?"

Gilda raised her hand, brought it quickly down upon the table, then said, "I told you a hundred times, this is not for me."

"Could we please listen, at least, to the rest of the crowd? Really, Gilda," snapped Mendel.

"For me, the jury is still out. I don't know," said Morris. "On the one hand, maybe we would all love it. But, what if we didn't? This could ruin us and the business would fall in the toilet, too, if it turned out we really could not stand each another."

"Spoken like a true capitalist, Moishkie. I knew it was in you," said Mendel. "I don't think it will affect our luck and profits one bit. In fact, an extra opinion here or there might make a world of difference."

"What are you, some kind of commie socialist? You so sweet you want to share just about everything?" questioned Morris.

Zena, pain causing her to squirm, finally spoke up. "My broken hip tells me I need people around me now and more later. Not that this is a complete disaster," she patted her side. "I will play shuffleboard again, but no more running. It's clear enough that we have to memorize each other's habits and routines. I got a bigger problem, if you want to know," she said.

"Well?" prodded Mendel.

"Outside, there's snow, ice, slush, and I cannot take two steps without thinking this will be the end of me. And, it will only get worse. I need heat all the time. Florida, California, some place like that."

"You're suggesting we pack and move, Zena?" asked Morris.

" I would rather Florida where we at least know someone."

"Not another move," said Gilda. "I'm just getting used to this. First, we live in Florida. Mind you, not in one spot, since you (gesturing to Zena) got ants all over. They make you hop from one spot to the next. Then, we are all split up and I'm on Long Island. Not for long since Springfield, it turns out, is the place to be. Now she wants me to go back to the South. Don't get me wrong. I hate this weather, too, but throwing all we own in one big basket, togetherness like that is not my idea of a good joke. Besides, stuff is scattered all over the place. I was just getting interested, already, in these three phases or whatever you call it. Me, I'm not going. No, and the idea of some kind of commune doesn't send chills up and down my spine either."

The outburst silenced all, but only momentarily. Gilda was embarrassed for having spoken from her heart, for having released a tiny voice inside her. Before anyone could respond, she became defensive. "I didn't mean to upset anyone. Maybe in the long run,

Florida looks like a great idea. I just can't see myself getting there, not at this age."

Mendel rapped his gnarled knuckles on the table. "Listen all of you, Gilda, Zena, and Morris," he said, nodding his head up and down. "I have an idea."

"Just what we need, another brainstorm," Morris said.

"Compromise. You started Phases. I suggest we go on vacation. Use it as a trial. We do well, we move in together. Not so good, no go."

Zena squirmed forward, Gilda raised both eyebrows, and Morris picked his cuticles, annoying everyone. Mendel continued, "We could go to St. Thomas, Bermuda, even Puerto Rico, I hear, is reasonable."

"For once you got something," said Zena.

"I will go," said Gilda, "at least we can look forward to warm sun on our backs."

"Not so bad," said Morris, " but where and how. We better get to work on it this minute!"

"I got friends all over, even in the travel business, which is not so good after the last few years. People are still afraid. Maybe a cruise, even," said Mendel.

"Now, you're talking big time," said Morris, who, circling the table, began to prance like a bear learning to waltz. He took Gilda by the crook of her arm while Mendel carefully ushered limping Zena about.

"Watch it, I'm just out of the hospital," cautioned Zena.

"Listen, I can take care of you better than any man ever could," said Mendel.

"You're proud to make such a statement?" she asked.

They spent the next twenty minutes sashaying around the room, exhausting themselves as they retold jokes they had heard on television or even radio, back to the early days before TV. Zena needed one of the men on each side of her to navigate her way to the car. Mendel was left with the mandate to quickly report back to the group on prospective cruises, complete with details relative to accommodations and itinerary. Suddenly, the success of the business had become secondary.

CHAPTER 10

It wasn't quite so simple for Mendel to manufacture a travel plan. But he relished the thought of haggling with an ancient crone of a travel agent. Mendel waited at the office of his longtime financial advisor, the lawyer Rubin, whom he formerly called a friend. Mendel needed to come up with a quick ten thousand dollars to secure the group vacation. He was enthusiastic enough that he did not even consider reimbursement. Mendel knew he had the money, at least on paper. What with the market's two-year downturn, he wondered about liquidating now and getting the cash. Ruby advised him to wait. He urged Mendel to hold steady. Ruby would not jeopardize Mendel's fiscal security – not even for a few bucks – not at this stage of life.

Morris was crushed by the news and urged Mendel to reconsider. "I will pay you back, I promise you, with double interest, just as soon as the business begins to roll." They had begun to equip the café. That component, they hoped, would support Phase II. Appliances were arriving and installation had begun. Where to situate easy chairs and the coffee bar? No decision was easily achieved.

Planning had been a breeze but actual positioning brought out the worst in the M&M boys.

Mendel was especially dour. "Listen," he said, "you just get outta town. You got no eye for this. Let me take care of it."

"Like hell I will. This place is my baby, my idea from the very first moment. You're lucky you're in on it, no less as a partner.

"My money does my talking. If you are not happy, walk away. I will make the final decisions," said Mendel, picking his teeth.

"Oh, you're upset about money again, now I get it. What is it this time?" asked Morris.

Mendel changed the subject. "Why set up this place now when in two weeks or a little longer we will fly off and go on vacation? What are the two of us doing?"

"It takes some time, my friend, to set up and outfit a business. This is just one small step in that great scheme of events."

"At this point, all we can take is small steps. Look." He inched forward, barely lifting his heels off the ground. "Look at you, you're fixing this place like we'll all live not till a hundred but at least ten, twelve years beyond that. We don't really know if we will survive the cruise. One of us might go or we could end up hating each other."

"Death, my friend, is not on my menu – not on any agenda or any note card I have."

"So, you think you'll live forever? That word mortality has never entered your mind?" asked Mendel, raising both of his arms.

Morris dropped the love seat he was lugging around. With the back of one hand, he wiped the sweat off his high forehead. "Mendel, when it happens, that's the end of everything. Over and out. No more arguments, no more frustrated love affairs – real or in our dreams. Sure, I think about it." He zeroed in and glared at his friend's eyes. "Tell me, though, what good does it do you to constantly bring this up? We live, we die, that is all. We cannot do one thing about the entrance and the exit. Only the middle, this long middle, is worth it. We have survived until now which means we can still have some fun."

"For once, you're probably right, but that does not help me. I can't help but stew about it all the time. You wonder why I'm in such a state, now you know. The store, the trip, these girls, everything has me in a tizzy. I forgot, even, why we're going away in the first place."

"Mendel, is this life a good thing or were we better off six, eight months ago when we really did not have much reason to live? Just answer that one for me and don't think about it too long."

Mendel turned his head so that Morris could not see the tears in his eyes. "I liked being young," Mendel said, burying his face in his hands.

***

It was mid-February when the foursome flew from Hartford to Fort Lauderdale. The idea was to spend an overnight in south Florida before boarding the cruise ship. Zena knew that a longer stay on land would prompt her to unpack and settle in. She so missed the old lifestyle. Better not think about those days, she told herself. Mendel had telephoned ahead to hold two rooms near the airport. True to form, he found the accommodations dingy, unattractive, in every way a disappointment.

"This is a dump, what with two rooms next to the laundry. We'll be up all night hearing machines, smelling exhaust, waiting for burglars. What are we, hired help?" asked Mendel.

"Mendel, just because someone's not Jewish, that doesn't mean he cannot function or be a person's friend," said Gilda. "Further, you found this motel."

Zena added, "We have to do better with the four of us right here. God knows we cannot control anything out there – in the world. Maybe my sister, at some point, had dreams. I have more today, in old age, I admit, than earlier."

The next morning, with scheduled stops in St. Thomas, Martinique, Aruba, Barbados, and the Panama Canal, they were ready to sail the seas. The women were far more optimistic, at least in comparison to their male counterparts.

"Will you look at that?" Morris asked, to no one in particular, but in a voice loud enough so that a dozen people or more could hear him. "This will be the last we see of land for, well, maybe forever."

"Keep your feeling to yourself, if you don't mind," said Zena.

"Let the big man speak," said Mendel. "If you even once studied Sigmund Freud, you would know that the sea is free, not bounded like the dirt of this earth."

"Since when are you the college professor?" asked Gilda. "One minute, you're preparing for the grave, the next you're talking like some fancy, educated big shot about psychology."

They stood together on the promenade of the Fair Princess as the boat gradually moved off into the expansive blue ocean. Suddenly, as if sneaking up from behind, a voice, friendly, loud, and polished, as in resonant radio, reverberated:

"Welcome one and all, to the Fairest Princess of them all. Just a tad late for breakfast today but for those of you desiring coffee and doughnuts, you are right on time. Find them, courtesy of the house, within the leeward dining room. Consult, if you will, your deck plan guide for directions. The Shore Touring Office is open from eight-thirty till eleven for land excursion details. Inquiries? Do not hesitate to ask. Religion? Each morning at ten o'clock, Cantor Ben Slokowsky will conduct services in the American Room. Carrying a bit extra weight around the middle? I hear no responses. Must mean everyone's in perfect shape. Just in case you wish to neutralize some of our gourmet meals, Jim Caddy will hold 'Fun In The Sun' fitness classes before lunch, say eleven-thirtyish on deck. Besides, we have a complete health spa, swimsuits recommended, down below in Whaler's Lounge. Bookish? Garrick Library is open all day. Game equipment is available until midnight at Mallard. Still with me or half asleep? All of this info, in case you chose to doze, is available at any of our three dining rooms. Tomorrow, incidentally, at ten, noon, and two, we'll be presenting 'Under Water' – a slide show for anyone intrigued with snorkeling and even scuba for the very daring. Morning activities always: board games and, I wish I could sing 'If I Were a Rich Man.' Shuffleboard, too. Harps or AARPS? The video which tells all of us how to prevent heart disease and stroke appears often on the large screen. Later in the week, our models will reveal the latest in bathing attire but we'll fill you in on that one closer to the time. Now, who's lost?"

"What is this, a hotel on water? I thought we booked a boat here," yelled Mendel, realizing as he spoke that he was not, as he hoped, making light of the situation. Everyone, instead, stared directly at him.

Morris talked to Mendel, "I'm with you on this one, Greenbaum. Before we even sit down and get a drink or two, they're hockin' and clockin' about fat and heart attacks."

Gilda jiggled the big man's belly, which rolled forward and over his belt. "A lot of good your diet's doing you," she said. "Your stomach has taken on a life of its own."

"Shush," he ordered, putting his index finger to her lips.

"Excuse me," the cruise leader continued, "but you need to know that lunch will be served in either the leeward or windward dining room. Give yourself thirty minutes before you swim or hit the track or get in some tennis. Those looking to read should find the bookstore, with both new and used. We have specialists here: one who teaches speed reading techniques, another a card trick artist, and we just discovered that one of our musicians is also a recently licensed hypnotist. Wannabe dancers can enroll in tango class. All of this is spelled out for you at Captain's Cabaret. Afternoons we leave fairly free. But, remember, we spend time each day ashore for shopping.

"Then, you'll want to wind down and maybe indulge in a drink or two before dinner. Each lounge has its own special ambience. We vary the music: soft pop/rock in one; a bit of New Orleans jazz in the other. Go north or south to reach the rooms – you're really making a circle. Dinner is served from six o'clock till just past eleven (they won't kick you out is what I mean) in the dining rooms. We leave munchies around for those truly in need. Tonight we feature Max Perling and his band in the Caribbean Hut – soft, romantic music but with a beat. No cover, all invited. Teenagers would no doubt prefer the Watering Hole, which comes complete with disco, rock, hip-hop, and whatever else they call the motion dances. Finally, we have not forgotten card sharks or plain old Bingo addicts. Even we, on the crew, get invited to play cards now and again.

"Those still wide awake can catch square dancing nightly, almost nightly, at ten or so. Tuckered out? Watch for Robert Redford Retrospective films such as 'Butch Cassidy,' 'The Candidate,' 'The Way We Were,' and 'All the President's Men.' No, not on the same night.

Bars stay open until two in the morning. And, as I said, there's plenty of food. They keep restocking the buffet in the Windward Room.

"That about does it for now. I have already listed many more hours than you can possibly handle. Again, the daily schedule is available at breakfast. And I am Zach Ginsler, your social director."

"I will say that is more than enough for a month. Some social director, he makes a big fat fool of himself," said Mendel. "For half his salary, I could do twice the job," he added.

"Mendel, don't criticize. If you don't stop, this trip will be murder," said Gilda.

"I been around. I know what goes on here. This is just the beginning of something which, so help me Gilda, stinks to high heaven," he said.

Morris broke his silence. "You watch your own steps and don't worry about everyone else."

The comment caught Mendel off-guard and he immediately thought of Lucy, someone who could show up anywhere unannounced. Never had he spoken one word about her to Morris. Maybe Morris knew and told Zena who might have blabbed to a roomful of people Mendel had never met. Mendel began to sweat profusely. "Not one word," he said to Morris.

The vacation passed by without incident. Morris gorged himself and put on a dozen pounds. His waistline disappeared entirely. Zena ate less but chose not to exercise. She, too put on weight. Gilda remained thin as a doorpost and Mendel, noshing regularly, held the line. His acidic stomach caused him to wince in pain with every bite he took. Each remained rooted to habit. Morris and Mendel played shuffleboard, swam immediately thereafter, and bet paltry sums of money on gin rummy at night. Gilda read – magazines, fiction, history books...whatever she could find. Zena continued to busy herself with needlepoint. She also hid Hershey's Kisses beneath sofa cushions. The sisters stayed away from one another but were far from secretive. Not a word was uttered about the future, a topic absolutely taboo.

The holiday passed without incident and they were soon back in Springfield. Mendel and Gilda returned to the duplex while Morris and Zena remained in the house on the other side of the park. As March slid into April the days grew thankfully longer, remains of snowfalls past melted and Morris stepped up his pace accordingly. Phases, suddenly, began to take shape. The café was soon ready for business but Morris wanted all three rooms set before staging a gala opening. Phase III, including state-of-the art shuffleboard courts which needed daily care and attention, was nearly complete. Morris searched for a perfect synthetic base – one with give and, he imagined, feeling. He wanted the solidity of asphalt but the texture of hardened clay. Why not humanize the playing surface to match the participants' emotions? He envisioned a sympathetic shuffleboard court designed for aging yet passionate athletes.

Mendel supervised installation. Without consulting others, he ordered the court painted deep coral, with bright white numbers and trim to offset. In addition, Mendel asked for studio lights, complete with individual dimmer switches for each bank of lamps. The lamps could provide extra warmth during frigid winter days but would remain shut down as sunlight flooded Phase III during long, platinum summer afternoons. Mendel sought finished, stained, handcrafted oak panels to function as outer walls.

The central community room, a gathering spot, remained problematic. Morris had trouble figuring just what to stock in what now seemed a vast space. He wanted necessities but frowned upon the gentrified, up-scale tone and texture he saw whenever he visited the trendy spots in hip Northampton, a half-hour's drive north. He could not list many inventory items that seemed satisfying. He knew Phase II was the guts – the soul of the place. Morris disregarded Mendel's early input -- just as well since Mendel would suddenly claim lack of interest. Throughout his life, whenever he felt slighted, the smaller man backed away, seemingly apathetic but covertly hurt.

Morris, dismayed with his own scarce imagination and matching low-level expertise, wanted Zena's opinion. Her facial features hardened and sharpened when she organized something – anything, the JCC Shuffleboard players, for example. Morris needed her to quickly raise funds for him. Barely able to admit, even to himself, his affection for her, he was reluctant to aggressively seek her advice. He was embarrassed to pursue her. Besides, it took courage. He was brought up to believe that men knew best. If he solicited Zena's help, this could be construed as a weakness. But, by whom?

He found himself leaving the store early on one unseasonably mild March afternoon as Mendel busied himself hanging photographs and paintings. Mendel had it in mind to create a small gallery, one which would showcase artists' work. Still, he never verbalized the notion and was certain no one was on to the plan. Meanwhile, Morris and Zena were meeting in the park.

Zena had amplified her volunteer activities at the Jewish Community Center. Her hip, never to be perfect again during this lifetime, remained serviceable. Her distance walking now limited, she turned, instead, to swimming. Always well-coordinated, she found lap activity hypnotic and could not wait to get herself back in the pool. Although she had shed fifteen pounds before falling, she packed that on and more by munching on chocolate covered cherries each afternoon during convalescence. Now, however, she began, once again, to lose. She had always been able to drop weight; each time, however, she had gained it back.

Morris sat on a solid, concrete park bench, thankful for occasional wooden slats supporting his back – a long stone's throw from Snowball the Polar Bear's cage. The unfortunate animal had been found poisoned years earlier. It seemed such a mystery and daily walkers, each disbelieving, ignored the cage, as if the beloved ball of fur might yet return. No one knew who committed the crime and no one investigated. Some suspected park officials, those responsible for feeding the ancient bear. It would have been simple to put an end to the messy animal.

Snowball and Morganetta, the scary elephant, were the last vestiges of a once classy Forest Park Zoo. Morganetta, sold to a Los Angeles facility, did not survive the year in southern California where, renamed Moduc, she succumbed to the artifices of life in Orange County.

Morris looked around and realized that the park, which he had long considered his own, was sliding away. Rotten garbage dotted the grandstand. Debris gathered but was never fully removed. Zoo animals died but were rarely replaced. Society farmed out its elderly – humans and animals alike. Buildings decayed, fell apart, or were leveled to the ground.

Money, Morris long thought, was the lone equalizer. You could not buy immortality but spending the next half or full life in a luxurious tomb was not out of the question. It took some means to preserve quality of life in old age. Aged men and women struggled to remain independent to avoid institutional care. Morris had some cash but not enough to last forever. He could not bear to consider where he might end up.

Now, four years after September eleventh, the image of planes smacking into the trade centers still haunted him. Some nights, he lay awake in fear. Morris found himself muttering, "Dust to dust, dirt to dirt, beneath tons of scrap metal and building parts? Not me." He pawed the ground with a long branch, dropped his head, and permitted his body to rock forward.

Zena saw him before he realized she was approaching. "Mo, something is wrong?" she asked. Morris lifted his head and realized that she was beautiful. Her short white hair had been pushed back from her forehead and her face was unlined. She was still glistening – having done several laps in the pool before bicycling to the park. Drops of water remained on her nose, between her eyes. Morris thought she might live another fifty years.

"Zena, I am one depressed old man."

"Yeah, you look it. So, what's the problem?"

"I don't know if I can go into that store we have created, day after day, week after week. I will sit there but will I get anything accomplished? I take boxes of hats that come in, put them on a shelf. Next time, I move them around. What's the difference? What is the purpose?"

"You want some help organizing? You turned to the right girl," she said.

"A little bit I could use," he said in a monotone.

"You are one sweet man, Mo. When it comes to running something, you know nothing. No wonder you never made any money. You start with a good system," she said, emphasizing with her hands. "You get yourself a three color sign, with some lighting on it, American even....Something like: Three Phases of Life. Has a ring to it, wouldn't you say?"

"Sounds like a book or a cheap movie, like we used to go and see at the drive-ins, if you ask me."

"Cheap this is not and maybe even interesting. So, what is wrong with that?"

"Aside from the fact that I should have thought of it, nothing."

"Next, you need to figure what people want. You've shown me that list six or seven times. Not one thing catches my eye. You want knick-knacks or health aids? Which will sell better and which should sell better? What will stand apart?"

"Both," said Morris, refusing to answer the question.

"What about people who want to sell their own goods here?

"Zena, I don't want no second-hand clothing store here."

"Well, if you really want variety, you could sell by consignment, too."

"Not a bad idea at that."

It took the better part of April to ready the store for business. Constantly referencing a mock-up Zena composed, Morris made certain the large sign was created to match the specifications she assigned. Zena insisted upon smaller, separate areas for each of the three phases. Mendel, surprisingly acquiescent, participated with great enthusiasm and little complaint.

Gilda, though, chose to abstain. She did enroll in two computer courses, correctly intuiting that state-of-the-art knowledge and dexterity with electronic media would expedite each process and task. Always a worrier, she now secretly fretted that she wouldn't retain all of the material. She, rather than the others, classified herself as a complete and dismal failure. Gilda spent extra hours at a community college where she found one sympathetic professor who would teach her individually, after class. Gradually, she began to solve the mystery within these machines. This was good but she sensed the time away was creating distance. Her friends remained in the shop while she was behind a terminal.

More positively, she began to take a liking to Springfield. Gilda had not previously been able to visualize an upside – why, she asked herself, are we so committed to western Massachusetts? That perception was beginning to soften, blur, and fade.

The winter, late in arrival but long-lasting, all but eradicated hope for a bountiful spring. A sudden blast of summer heat and humidity enveloped the region in mid-April. Morris and Mendel, who had chosen May 1st for the grand opening, took this as an ominous sign. The sizzling weather, however, was short-lived. Zena placed ads in local papers and major television stations listed Phases in calendars. Mendel, wearying of his usual, contentious role, paid the bill without questioning the math.

Gilda saw herself as an emissary and she permeated the community, spreading word of Phases. The harder she worked, the more invigorated she felt. She argued herself into believing the aging process could be slowed, interrupted. Associating with younger people was key. She began to consider the virtues of a longer life. Never before had the concept intrigued her. She became convinced that exhausting rather than bypassing each moment was the way to go. Each time the sisters saw one another they embraced. Each understood the precious quality of moments together. Zena and Gilda compared notes on men. Zena thought about the possibility of developing one shuffleboard team to travel, another of mothers and daughters; she wondered about an intra-Springfield league. Gilda entered data, having bought herself a new laptop computer and, with the good graces of both Mendel and Morris, a flat screen special for the office. She sat in her chair and spun about, making faces at all comers.

CHAPTER 11

Newly motivated, Gilda gladly assumed duties as office administrator, phone receptionist, and secretary. She had grand schemes and began by contacting senior citizen groups thirty minutes away. Why wouldn't people from Northampton, even Amherst and perhaps the Hartford region, as well, come to visit for a day? While her friends insisted Gilda must be senile to encourage the elderly to shlep so far, she countered by insisting that old people were lonely and desperate. Given incentive, they would travel. Changes of scene worked invigorating wonders. Gilda thought of herself when she spoke. Secretly, Gilda imagined creating a comforting center with books, films, music, and relatively inexpensive food and drink. She knew she could cajole others in her age group to at least give it a try. After all, these people were starving for culture and entertainment.

Morris was busy. He wanted to celebrate the opening with a parade from the park to the new store. He argued park officials into sectioning off a street lane – space enough for them to make the one mile trek together. Opening day finally arrived and with it a cool breeze. Prognosticators promised sunshine by ten in the morning.

Joggers were delighted to find traffic stalled as motorists sat impatiently. One runner saluted Morris, the man he correctly guessed to have engineered the slowdown.

Mendel and Gilda remained at the store, reasoning that possible patrons might head there first. It was important to have greeters, to extend a warm invitation.

Morris and Zena, meanwhile, positioned themselves equidistant from several baseball diamonds. Just after eleven o'clock that morning, the city's all-volunteer, rarely rehearsed, but dedicated and enthusiastic marching band arrived on the scene. In-line skaters, dog walkers, young parents with infants in strollers all stopped to listen. The turnout was embarrassingly meager. Suddenly, however, a good twenty people appeared, surrounding a shocked Morris and Zena.

Motorists, out of curiosity, stopped their cars. Others had planned a trip to the park. Morris was dumbfounded but Zena played it cool. For many days, she had exuded confidence, assuming or pretending to be convinced that all would be well. She made the foolish prediction that they might have fifty or sixty in attendance.

Zena took Morris's hand and led him onto the podium as a long, sleek, low vehicle made the turn from the skating arena toward the green field.

"That's a Connecticut car," said Zena. "Gilda and her advertising brought us at least one customer. Good enough, I'll take it!"

One by one, a contingent of mostly frail, elderly women stepped tentatively out of the car, onto the pavement. As they did, the driver stuck her head out the window, trying to get Morris's attention. She chewed a wad of pink gum, evident each time she blew a large bubble. Her auburn red hair spread over her eyes as the wind whipped through her locks. She pushed at her hair, trying to stuff it beneath her Yankees cap. She encouraged her passengers who were anxious when it came to descending the steps. Suddenly, she twirled, bounced, and came to a jump stop in front of Morris. He recognized the face and form but could not quite find a context.

She walked right up to Morris, leaned into his face, and grazed his forearm lightly with hers. "Where's Mendel, honey?" she asked. Morris's blush ran from the folds of his neck through his hairline.

"Pardon me, Miss, but how do you come to know my friend, Mendel?"

"Don't you just tell me you forgot the shape of this little, well, this body? And (she removed her hat, shaking loose an abundance of thick, streaked hair), I've been told once you spot my mane you don't forget it, 'specially if you're a man. Which you are." A crowd of onlookers, including senior citizens and passers-by, had assembled.

"I know you but where, God help me, I cannot say. This gets worse with each passing week. Unless I write something down, it's gone. Call this what you wish – what I know is that it is one, damn nuisance."

Zena stepped up at that moment. "Oh, so you know this, this young, tart thing? Well, then you got some explaining to do, to me, Mo."

"I don't forget faces, that is all, Zena." His voice was surprisingly small and unassuming.

"Lucy or Lacy whichever it is, that's you," said Morris, his face suddenly gleaming.

"With the long e at the end, either way," she added "The Holiday Inn. Richmond. Come on, sugar," she implored, with a touch of impatience. "These days I'm a Connecticut worker who drives around old folks for a living."

"You will just have to excuse me for one moment," he said, putting his arm around Zena's shoulders and ushering her toward the brick house.

"You and your nerve," scolded Zena, resisting his pull. As soon as they were out of earshot, she added, "Messing with a teenager, you think you're Mr. Big or something? Where, do tell me, did you meet that floozy?"

"Mendel."

"Mendel?"

"On the way to the tournament in Florida, before we hit the jackpot and found the loves of our lives, the Lewis sisters."

Zena's mouth dropped open. She was temporarily stifled but allowed Morris to gently steer her and they ambled in the direction of the crowd. Lucy stared at him, glared at him but he tried to remain suave and cool, tending to the business at hand. He neither honored nor avoided her gaze. After all, she was a supplier – of potential patrons, another market in the offing. What personal business she had with Mendel, well, that is his problem, not mine, thought Morris. Let him proceed and Mendel would deal with fallout – or perhaps not.

Just before noon, the band played "You're a Grand Old Flag" and the procession began. Everyone marched, raggedly, and soon departed through the newly refurbished main entrance of the park, along Sumner Avenue, heading east. Classic, clichéd tunes filled the air as off key attempts at "When the Saints Go Marching In" and "I'm a Yankee Doodle Dandy" highlighted the walk. Someone began whistling "Colonel Bogie's March" and others, off-pitch and without rhythm, followed suit. They ambled, stumbled, limped along, each to his own style and pace, until everyone finally arrived at the new store. About one hundred yards to the right a banner flew gently, proclaiming: "Phases I II III – For Mature Individuals -- Community and Café – Shops and Services." The M&M boys thought this had some ring to it. They smiled at one another.

Decked out in a cream-colored, pinstriped sport jacket complemented by a soft- peach ascot, Mendel stood by the shop eagerly awaiting the first curious souls. Gilda, at his side, held and twirled pompoms of red, white, and blue, her own creations.

Automobile pick-up and delivery was available for those who knew the walk would completely exhaust them. Morris carefully instructed all motorists to drive around the park periphery. He advised, then threatened them not to exit through the main gate. A few early birds who began but could not finish were picked up by minivans which were just arriving on site. Everyone seemed glad to be there. The universe was in tune. Morris thought the timing to be exquisite. For this, he took full credit.

Mendel and Gilda embraced. Morris and Zena, taking the hint, paired off and hugged, as well. The sun's shiny, luminous rays further glorified the festivities. Mendel squinted hard and while shielding his eyes from the sun realized that a Lucy! - was making eyes at him. He didn't know what to do. Mendel marched directly and purposefully toward the front door at Phase I. "Let me show everyone around. If you haven't seen our place or even if you have, won't you please join me," he called. Many followed, including Lucy. Mendel took a deep breath and admitted to himself as he exhaled that she was drop-dead gorgeous. She stayed loyal, though, to her Hartford-based entourage.

Mendel attempted to shy away from Lucy, whom he found physically irresistible. He could not suppress his desire and, sweating at the brow, surreptitiously dabbed at his forehead. He really wished, in part, that she would vanish. She, however, did not and he grew more anxious with each passing moment. Any sort of public disclosure, including even a veiled reference to his past dalliance with Lucy, could not be risked. Zena and Gilda were nearby and Mendel feared the very worst.

He chose to distract and busy himself, bending low to demonstrate the elasticity of the shuffleboard playing surface in Phase III. Lucy took advantage to edge closer to him. "My, what a splendid coating," she said. "Could I have my own demonstration?" She took him by the wrist.

"Best in the northeast is what they tell me," he said. "Try it out yourself, Miss."

"In case you didn't know, I brought that van of people in from Hartford," she said. "I work with old folks now."

"That comes as no surprise whatsoever," pronounced the smirking Mendel as she straightened up. Then he addressed Lucy's group. "I hope you will come back. You see, we (he pointed first at his chest, then at them) have nothing like this. You don't live close enough to stop in every day, but once a month?" His face relaxed into a smile, revealing dimples, creases, and cracks.

Lucy pressed a wad of paper into Mendel's palm. "You dropped this," she fibbed. "It slid out of your pocket when you were showing us the floor." She touched Mendel's wrist again, then held his hand before releasing with a slight tug. Lucy then walked slowly back to her place with the Connecticut contingent.

Mendel shoved the paper in his pocket and was less than astonished to feel aroused and hard. As delighted as he was embarrassed, he stood. Only this woman, among many, could enliven him so. Smug and happy, he chortled to himself.

"Excuse me, I need the facilities," he explained to his audience. "If anyone, well, when others need them, too, they are at the rear of the café, Phase II, next partition over. And, be assured we make them most accessible."

Mendel yanked the stall door closed, pressed himself down, and massaged. Soon enough, he was limp and normal. Satisfied, he relieved himself, zipped up, straightened the remains of what were once his shoulders, skipped away from the toilet, washed his hands thoroughly with detestable chemical soap and, by chance, caught his image in the mirror before him.

He watched as his eyelids, taking on lives of their own, fluttered, danced, and twitched. All this for one unattainable shiksa, he thought? Just because he and his fat friend could poke disks around on a shuffleboard court? This could not possibly be a part of any god's divine plan. Or, maybe this was a sign, a summons for the grim reaper to take Mendel away. Like an unsolicited phone call, even a clunky, out-of-date answering machine message. High tech, shmi-tech, he thought to himself, mortality was surely the issue here. Despite the implications, Mendel felt a pull, a force. He leaned on the sink and pondered the past.

His childhood, no, he could not visualize clearly enough. Images, true. Wearing his roller skates and latching onto the rear end of garbage trucks. Taking the subway up and back, up and back, sometimes getting off at Yankee Stadium to watch the Babe wolf down franks and smack a few homers. Still, the pictures blurred and, what's more, Mendel had no desire to separate the images. Let them be.

No, he didn't care what he looked like when he was eight or ten or fifteen. His kids, though, and Hester, they pushed themselves into view. Since he and Morris had left for Florida, nearly a year ago, he had barely kept in touch with the children. He thought only occasionally of his wife. Yes, she was dead maybe eight years but he used to have her with him every moment. Each memory sustained him. Now?

When he and Gilda were on Long Island, yes, the kids, the grandchildren came to visit. Mendel now realized he hadn't taken the time to focus, to pay attention. Gilda received letters from friends, from cousins in Florida. Morris and Zena? Yes, they seemed to care about family. Nothing more than routine, but something.

Mendel realized that for too long a time he had deceived himself by playing games with his past. He treated his youth and even middle age as if these were forgotten years, lost in time. Yet, names and faces crept into his consciousness. Sometimes, he could not discriminate between those still living and others long gone. On those rare occasions when he attempted to delineate, the memories were too distorted to fully decipher and he grew frustrated and disoriented. Better and less painful to forget.

Now, in need of instruction, he faced forward and stared at the withered old man before him in the glass. This was his life and these lips were still moving. Mendel promised himself that he would face -- seek the future, regardless of life expectancy tables. If young Lucy could jolt his pulse and bring his blood to full boil, why check out early? After all.....

Mendel's resolve solidified. Self-imploring, he gathered himself, recalling topflight athletes he had seen on television, steadied himself to strut out of the restroom and prepared to meet and greet expectant patrons. His close friends gathered and waited, fully expectant. Mendel, his mind working overtime, assigned adjectives: Beloved Morris, loyal Zena, precious Gilda. All shone with renewed radiance, as if wearing stage make-up. No one, however, knew what Mendel might say. Mendel worried that he could inadvertently become offensive. On the other hand, he urgently needed to establish himself as a man of integrity.

"Lucy," he called and waved. "Lucy, these are my people. And this is Lucy." Morris nodded knowingly, then winked at Mendel. The men nodded at one another.

His self-esteem on the ascent, Mendel continued, "She is my great niece from Virginia. First time for her to be here in Springfield, second time in this Commonwealth. I thought I might take her for a walk through our park." Mendel spread his arms high and wide, as if to lead a congregation.

Morris, wishing to affirm, raised his arm and pointed to Mendel. Zena shrugged awkwardly, opened her mouth, but did not speak.

"Excuse us then," said Mendel, taking one of Lucy's hands and strolling off. As they approached the front door, he turned and said to all who might listen, "She's beautiful, that's what we all know. Take my word."

Mendel ushered Lucy out the door. Side by side, they slowly walked toward the park along Dickinson Street. Mendel wondered whether this was actually named for the poet. They crossed onto

Trafton Road, the rear entrance to the park coming into view. Mendel removed the folded paper from his pocket. Shielding his eyes from the sun's glare, he read, moving his lips so as to become barely audible: "Mendel, you were right. Money isn't everything. Take some time and please show me around someday? I would like that. You are one of the nice men. Lucy."

She must have dropped that guy, thought Mendel – the one with more money even than me. So she likes me and what am I to do? I don't really know. She likes me and this is a good thing. That is all.

"Lucy, dear, this park of more than seven hundred acres was designed by a man named Frederick Law Olmsted. You know Central Park in the Big Apple? That is a perfect and fitting example of what a mensh he was." She tilted her head to one side; Mendel remembered the gesture. She was cute, like a puppy. "I mean he was a smart, honorable, upstanding man."

"Right," she said, slowly. "Sure. You positive it was Olmsted?"

"We had some zoo here, you should have seen it. Lions, tigers, elephants. A sight fit for a king or queen. I wish you could have been here."

By now, they were moving through the park and circling toward the ball field.

"Where are all the animals, Men?" she asked.

"We still got some, Lucy, but nothing like the very old days. Like us, they go somewhere else. I, though, am still here. You are, too. What else counts? Not necessarily better, certainly not worse. Just new, just different, just one old man and one lovely woman.

"I will remember you, Lucy, and I hope you will visit. Perhaps you will get to know me better, and my friends, too. If ever it rains for forty days and forty nights and a flood threatens the world, these people I know and love, we will all get on the ark together. With luck, Lucy, there will be space for you. But I have to tell you, Lucy. My friends come first."

THE END

ACKNOWLEDGMENTS

For their love, support, and assistance: Betsy, Jason, Scott, Nina and Ashley – my family.

For proofreading: Ann Jacobs.

For his belief in Mendel and Morris: Tom Hallock.

FRED SOKOL

ABOUT THE AUTHOR

Fred Sokol is currently Director of Theater Arts at American International College. He also reviews professional theater for talkinbroadway.com. Sokol is co-author of the book *Muses in Arcadia: Cultural Life in the Berkshires*. He lives in Longmeadow, Massachusetts with his wife, Betsy.

www.ingramcontent.com/pod-product-compliance
Lightning Source LLC
Chambersburg PA
CBHW071652090426
42738CB00009B/1504